School and System Leadership

Also available from Continuum

Developing a Self-Evaluating School, Paul K. Ainsworth
New Primary Leaders, edited by Michael Cowie
Understanding System Leadership, Pat Collarbone and John West-Burnham

School and System Leadership

Changing roles for primary headteachers

Susan Robinson

continuum

Continuum International Publishing Group

The Tower Building	80 Maiden Lane
11 York Road	Suite 704
London SE1 7NX	New York NY 10038

www.continuumbooks.com

British Library Cataloguing-in-Publication Data
A catalogue record for this book is available from the British Library.

ISBN: 978-1-4411-6399-8 (hardcover)
      978-1-4411-8684-3 (paperback)

Library of Congress Cataloging-in-Publication Data
A catalog record for this book is available from the Library of Congress.

Typeset by Newgen Imaging Systems Pvt Ltd, Chennai, India
Printed and bound in India

Contents

Part 3 **FINDINGS AND IMPLICATIONS FOR SCHOOL
LEADERSHIP AND GOVERNMENT POLICY**

Acknowledgement

Writing this book, while I hope it is of use and interest to others, is a hugely self-indulgent exercise which has impacted on the lives of others. I wish to acknowledge many people, but particularly my husband Graham for his patience, unconditional support and belief in me, which sustained me throughout.

Mike Bottery, Tony Bush and Richard Hatcher encouraged me to write this book and David Hopkins kindly offered to write the foreword. I am deeply grateful to them. Roy Blatchford, Mike Bottery, Megan Crawford and David Middlewood read drafts of the manuscript. I appreciate their honest and developmental feedback. Any mistakes are, of course, entirely mine.

I would like to express my gratitude to the staff and governors at Cherry Orchard School in Birmingham. In particular, I wish to acknowledge my appreciation of the personal and professional support from Fiona Wilson, Alison Taylor, Peter Harper, Sue Flannery and our Chair of Governors Clifford Fryer.

All the heads interviewed were unstinting in giving their time and willingness to engage with the research. It would have been impossible to write this book without them. I am grateful to all and in awe of their dedication and moral purpose to achieve the best education for children.

Foreword

During the winters of 2002–5, while Chief Adviser to the Secretary of State for School Standards, I took my Ministers on the road. The purpose was to encourage debate between Ministers and senior civil servants on the one hand, and headteachers on the other, over the development of education policy. This was a time, as Susan Robinson records in this detailed and insightful book, of significant shifts in the educational policy landscape. Although it was clear at the time that direct state intervention was necessary to raise standards when they were too low and too varied, some of us were beginning to question whether this was still the recipe for reform in the medium term. When progress begins to plateau – while a bit more might be squeezed out in some schools, and perhaps a lot in underperforming schools – I doubted that 'top down' change was still the answer. I began to feel that to ensure that every student reaches his or her potential, schools needed to lead the next phase of reform. The $64,000 question of course is how do we do that? It was this query that provided the subtext for the workshops.

As we began to discuss and negotiate quite significant shifts in policy – such as the introduction of personalized learning, the new relationship with schools, earned autonomy and forms of networked leadership – with what turned out to be many tens of thousands of headteachers, I began to discern a glimmer of an answer. What was so striking about this series of conversations over that three-year period in the mid-2000s was how far the work culture of Heads had changed from ten years earlier. The educational reforms of the late 1980s and 1990s had produced a competitive ethic between heads and their schools both Primary and Secondary. Our discussions during these workshops exhibited a dramatically different dynamic, one that was grounded in collaboration and a commitment to the progress of schools other than their own.

It is this shift from competition to collaboration, from individualism to systemic promise that Susan Robinson charts in this book. In so doing, she presents a textured account of the emergence of system leadership in Primary schooling in England over the past 20 years. As is so clearly demonstrated on the pages that follow, 'system leaders' care about and work for the success of other schools as well as their own. They measure their success in terms of improving student learning and increasing achievement, and strive to both raise the bar and narrow the gap(s). Crucially, they are willing to shoulder system leadership roles in the belief that in order to change the larger system you have to engage with it in a meaningful way.

There is little that I can add to the detailed and authentic analysis situated in the deep experience of our leading heads that Susan Robinson presents here. But there are three themes described in the book that are, in my experience, of particular importance and are worth highlighting.

First, that heads who have led their schools through a journey of improvement have followed a fairly consistent combination of strategies within and across three broad phases of success. In schools in more challenging contexts, greater attention and efforts are made in the early phase to establish, maintain and sustain school-wide policies for pupil behaviour, improvements to the physical environment and improvements in the quality of teaching and learning. In the middle phase, heads tend to expand leadership roles and responsibilities, emphasize curriculum breadth and make more regular and focused use of data to inform decision making about pupil progress and achievement. In the later phase, key strategies tend to relate to personalizing and enriching the curriculum, as well as wider distribution of leadership. It is also during this phase that heads, having successfully led their schools through an improvement process, want to share the experience of this success with other schools. This is the altruistic basis of system leadership.

Second, the emergence of system leadership roles presages a transformation in the landscape of the education system with a radical realignment of responsibilities. This is based on a growing recognition that schools need to lead the next phase of reform. The implication is, as I have already hinted, that we need a transition from an era of prescription to an era of professionalism – in which the balance between national prescription and schools leading reform will quite dramatically change. However, achieving this shift is not straightforward. We cannot simply move from one era to the other without self-consciously building professional capacity throughout the system. It is this task, as Susan Robinson so clearly demonstrates, that is assumed by our emerging breed of system leaders.

Third, there is also confirmation from the evidence in this book that there is a striking quality about fine teachers and school leaders – they care deeply about their students. Indeed, it is clear that system leadership as described on these pages is driven by a moral purpose that is determined to create the conditions for learning and teaching that enables every student to reach their potential. It is the expression of such a moral purpose that provides the narrative for improvement. This, in turn, puts a focus on the learning and teaching strategies that ensure success in student learning and achievement and builds powerful cultures for teacher learning that extends well beyond the boundary of the school.

Susan Robinson elaborates on these and many other important themes in this beautifully crafted exposition of her doctoral research. The result is a carefully woven contemporary history of school leadership that draws on the lived experience of many of our exemplary headteachers and develops propositions that will enable many more of our educational leaders to become similarly outstanding.

David Hopkins
Professor Emeritus, Institute of Education,
University of London
Formerly Chief Adviser to three Secretaries
of State on School Standards

Introduction

When speaking with headteachers, the conversation often develops along the lines of their changing role and the new opportunities they are being offered. These can be wide ranging but, increasingly, headteachers are being invited to lead in other more vulnerable schools as identified typically here:

> The idea is to create a chain of 4 or 5 schools over a two-year period and brand them with my current school branding. The LA [Local Authority] I work in is absolutely committed to federations and sees it as a very effective way of saving and improving schools which have been below floor targets for 6-9 years and which have usually had more headteachers than they should have had.' (headteacher Ht 27)

> 'In one of my schools the head had an Ofsted and came out of category but things were not good. Following a review and discussions the LA paid her off and she left. I went in there acting while they decided what to do. The other school which is now my second school had no deputy and another one of the leadership team had left and so they had a vacuum and the SATs were below floor targets for many years. There were a lot of issues. I ended up as the substantive head for both schools.' (Ht 19)

Never far from the minds of heads is the importance of maintaining high levels of pupil performance and validation of their leadership:

> I suppose it's keeping the momentum going after an 'outstanding' Ofsted . . . A lot is to do with your school's test results and we all know that they fluctuate. They are up and down and we have to manage not only the standards but all the other areas of education. So standards and maintaining our position is the big one for me. (Ht 8)

This book is the result of my journey to discover the impact of education policy on the role of the headteacher, from the point of view of the profession. The research uses the views of headteachers to examine to what extent they have the opportunity to manage education policy and develop it to suit their contexts and to what extent they are driven by statute or influence to comply.

During the course of the research, I found my own role was developing along similar lines to that of many of my colleagues. I was first involved working in other schools from 2002 by invitation of the local authority (LA). becoming a National Leader of Education (NLE) in 2007. While not using my own experience as a case study, my first-hand knowledge, together with a PhD which researched the changing role of the primary school headteacher, is a contributory factor to my understanding.

The international context

The book is written primarily for an English audience, as it researches the views of English headteachers (school principals). Diverse school systems interpret their educational challenges into policy and practice differently (Bottery, 2006). Nevertheless, the themes in this book have implications for a wider readership, as there are a number of themes and a degree of policy-borrowing common across many countries in the modern industrialized world as they respond to global challenges. Themes include the economic challenge of educating to develop the appropriate human resources for a knowledge economy (Spring, 2008). Another is the imminent retirement of the post-Second World War baby-boomer generation. Often accompanying this has been a dearth of interest shown by aspirant leaders to take up the challenge of becoming principals or headteachers (Pont et al., 2008). Policies have been developed to reshape school systems as a response to these issues.

Decentralized administrative structures have been introduced, offering a degree of autonomy for principals to lead. Their aim is to increase efficiency at the local level by making the schools or districts more responsive to the market. An increase in autonomy is also frequently accompanied by a centralizing of the curriculum, high-stakes testing and by an increase in school leaders being held to account for the performance of the schools they lead. Whether or not the curriculum is itself based on a common framework, the use of tests and monitoring procedures to assess the performance of students is common worldwide, for example the UK, Canada, Australia; USA, Sweden, Hong Kong and New Zealand.

Nationalising standards and tests is occurring not only within countries but also across many of them, allowing students' narrowly defined academic progress to be benchmarked internationally. The use of Progress in International Reading Literacy Studies (PIRLS), Trends in Mathematics and Science Study (TIMSS) and the Programme for International Students Assessment (PISA) are examples of the use of an international comparison to assess student performance.

The use of this policy is an example not only of the globalization of ideas, in this case of testing and assessment, but also the 'peer pressure' (Moos et al., 2008) which can result as a consequence of countries using the findings to compare their relative positions in an international league table of results. No matter how highly a country's school system achieves, there will always be room for improvement (Levin, 2010). This constant drive for higher performance has the potential to push schools to 'teach to the test' and for curricula to cover only the acceptable body of knowledge deemed necessary to produce a suitable workforce.

Greater autonomy in many devolved systems has also led to tight accountability where school leaders are accountable for the measurable outcomes of children's performance. This can also be accompanied by a system of inspection. The extent to which principals can manoeuvre themselves space within the expectations of accountability systems to act autonomously will inevitably differ from one country to another.

One concept adopted internationally is the virtue of training and developing school leaders, which helps to ensure their supply and effectiveness. Bush (2008b) identifies differences between leadership development in centralized and decentralized systems in developed countries. This is important to considerations relating to leadership succession. In centralized systems, succession is planned with the identification and preparation of potential candidates, together with a central determination of the criteria used to select them. The issue for decentralized systems, where self-management allows for local decisions, is that the choice to apply lies with aspirant leaders, with the inherent danger that not enough potential applicants will come forward.

In recent years, there has been an increase in the existence of institutions such as the Australian Institute for Teaching and School Leadership and The National College in England. Their purpose is to contribute towards improvements in the quality of teaching and school leadership and succession management. Both institutions commission research and develop training programmes to achieve this.

The need for an international standards or leadership framework has been raised (Caldwell and Paddock, 2008). The likelihood of an international system of standards presupposes that they are applicable in different countries. Dimmock and Walker (2000) have highlighted the problems inherent in transferring ideas without an understanding of how they will be translated in the context receiving them, as leadership is constructed differently according to context. Therefore, what may be admired in leadership in an English context, such as the leader who distributes leadership to others, may be seen as weak in another context that admires the heroic, singular leader.

Another difficulty in the spread of universal standards is that the development of leaders takes different forms. For some, there is access to nationally or regionally inspired leadership development, which, if delivered by national providers, could offer an approach which would align consistently with international standards. However, for more customised development such as that given by faith-based institutions or company sponsors, training may take a different approach to common issues.

The English context

Globalization in terms of its challenges, practices and ideas has had an impact on the introduction of English educational policy. There have been constant drives to raise the standards of students to ensure a workforce fit to service a knowledge economy and the impact of succession management due to the impending retirement of the baby boomers.

Decentralization and schools self-management have been accompanied by centralization of the curriculum and a national system of testing used to benchmark the performance of schools. While headteachers enjoy a degree of autonomy, it is earned through a system of rigorous accountability. The Office for Standards in Education, Children's Services and Skills (OFSTED) provides the process where headteachers are held accountable for the successful performance of their schools.

Given the centrality of headship in English schools (Southworth, 2008), effective school leadership is crucial. Calls for system redesign in the second term of the Labour government by many advisers and commentators, including Barber (2002) and Chapman (2002), were partly predicated on recognition of the importance of the role of the headteacher in leading and delivering the reforms in schools but also that this role, was itself, in need of reform. The aims of government in changing the role of head to help create a fit for purpose education system have led to opportunities for headteachers to undertake new roles across school systems through the use of system leadership. This involved the sharing of leadership knowledge and practices in collaborations, often school to school, and networks.

The coalition

The inconclusive general election in 2010 led to a coalition between the majority Conservative Party and the Liberal Democrats. It was perceived that the issues facing the government were similar to those being espoused by Labour in the need to raise standards to educate for a knowledge economy (DfE, 2010b). There was also the ongoing issue that baby boomers had yet to retire, with consequences for succession management.

A consistency in policy was recognition by the coalition of the benefits of using successful headteachers and other staff in their schools to transfer this success across the system by working to support schools vulnerable to failure. The coalition extended Labour's approach to system diversity by creating new school structures in the form of new types of academies converted firstly from outstanding schools together with free schools. Despite the strong drive towards localism and the philosophical move towards diversity and a self-improving system, the coalition has retained certain central mechanisms. These include, with some differences in their structure and process, the continued use and reform of the National Curriculum and OFSTED inspections.

Methodology

My perspective as a headteacher has contributed to the construction and articulation of findings gained from a range of semi-structured interviews with 27 headteachers from 14 local authorities in three rounds from 2005 to 2011. I have included the context of their roles in the appendix. Some contextual information, such as location, has been omitted, as it would potentially lead to the identification of some of the heads who have recognizable roles in their locality.

All the schools had at least good progress and usually, but not exclusively, high attainment. There was a range of schools according to local authority and context such as size of school and deprivation indicators within local authorities. Headteachers were chosen to ensure there was a range of experience, age and gender. They were sampled to fit the criteria through validation by OFSTED (as very good or excellent, pre-2005 or outstanding post-2005).[1]

---

1 The only exception was Ht 25 who had just undertaken a new headship of a rural federation and was chosen for context but hadn't undergone an Ofsted in the role having received a letter from HMCI to the effect that it would be delayed due to the context of the school. Post interview Ofsted graded leadership as outstanding.

In addition, a snowballing approach was used where the interviewees often suggested others. This occurred with reference to the executive headteachers, which was appropriate in a field where system leadership is comparatively new with few executive, academy or federated primary school leaders.

The research was limited to those who were deemed effective through inspection, not because this is the only judgement of effective headship but because it enables the study of the position of those whom the government consider can be trusted to implement its policies. It is, however, important to stress that while the government may trust those heads who have achieved an 'outstanding' rating, the interviewees include headteachers with a variety of views of the success of government policy, ranging from supportive, mildly critical and heavily critical of policy. For more detail, see Robinson (2009, 2011).

Format of the book

All the chapters are aimed at highlighting how policy, its impact and the challenges it has created for school leadership has affected the role of headteachers as they seek to manage transformational and systemic change. The book is divided into three parts and nine chapters. Part 1 consists of Chapters 1–3, Part 2 of Chapters 4–7 and Part 3 of Chapters 8–9.

Part 1 provides a picture of the landscape of school leadership in an English national context. While the focus of this book is more on how school leaders have managed change than a review of all the changes themselves, it is nevertheless important to understand the context in which school leaders work and the policy to which they are reacting. Chapter 1 considers the issues governments face when introducing policy. It identifies and analyzes the main themes of educational policy from 1944 to 2001. In addition, it gives the reasons why the leading policy advisers of the day at the beginning of the second term of the Labour government believed the system needed to change. It offers the reasons for, and the implications of, systems thinking on policy design. Chapter 2 discusses how the policies of the Labour government from 2001 and those introduced by the coalition in 2010 have led to changes to the role of headteachers. It discusses the challenges and opportunities for heads in single institutions and across schools as system leaders. Chapter 3 considers theoretical frameworks of leadership and the type of leadership and professional development offered to heads to understand the challenges and opportunities that affect them. It considers the role of the National College, arguably the most influential of all the leadership development trainers, as it manages the entry to headship in the form of National Professional Qualification for Headship (NPQH), designates NLEs and teaching schools.

Part 2 identifies the main challenges facing headteachers in England and analyzes how they manage their roles within the constraints of the current changing education system. Chapter 4 describes the headteachers understanding of change and the development of new roles. It considers their opinions about the centrality of their role in schools, their motivations and characteristics. This chapter traces the changes that have occurred in relationships with parents and governors, in particular, as a result of new roles for headteachers. Chapter 5 identifies the type of new external and internal roles being undertaken by headteachers as a result of their response to government policy and how their school/s have changed as an organization. Chapter 6 includes how headteachers manage their accountability and their pressure to maintain standards and the impact this had on their leadership and school organization. Chapter 7 considers how changes to the traditional role of headteachers required certain actions to be sustainable. It involves a discussion as to how headteachers are moving towards a more strategic role, using workforce reform and distributing their leadership.

Part 3 provides some conclusions from the analysis in Part 2 of the changing role of headship and implications and recommendations for government regarding the impact of educational policy for change. Chapter 8 identifies seven key findings from the perceptions and opinions of headteachers as they react to opportunities afforded them as a result of education policy. It offers some conclusions regarding the state of headship. Chapter 9 offers implications and recommendations for government regarding the implementation of its policy as it continues to develop the role of system leadership in the school system. Some themes are common and some responses from governments are generic in nature.

Part 1
Policy Contexts and the Challenges of Headship

The Changing Landscape of Headship: From Consensus to System Redesign

1

While conscious that this is not a historical book, to understand the changes which shape the role of the primary headteacher, it is useful to review the educational policy context and changes in ideology which have shaped the school system within which headteachers operate. This chapter considers how the introduction of educational policy is subject to various economic, political and social pressures. It then moves on to review the educational landscape and issues which existed before the second term of the New Labour government and prompted calls for system redesign.

Introducing education policy: issues to consider

There are forces which can be both national and international and are associated with the introduction of government policy and to which it must respond. These influences complicate its design and implementation.

Political influences

Governments in democratic countries need to please the electorate to be re-elected. Such a political dimension to reforms, however, doesn't necessarily make them educationally desirable (Levin, 2003). This can cause a tension for governments which seek to ensure both political and educational advantage. This could lead to governments either interpreting research findings in ways which suit their political motive, being selective in the studies they choose to use or ignoring them altogether.

National contexts

To transfer policies out of national context for use internationally can potentially cause difficulties in that the context in which the policies were originally formed may not be suitable for the purpose for which they are now intended (Levin, 2003). It may be that a policy's success in a particular country is more due to its cultural and economic systems than to the policy or practice itself (Bottery, 2007). The success of policy-borrowing in education may depend not just on context but also on the stage of development of an individual nation's school system. Mourshed et al. (2010, 3) identified a 'consistent cluster of interventions' which were different from each other but which characterized school systems moving on a continuum of performance. They identified commonality of interventions used by different education systems at the same stage of performance, which ranged from poor to fair, fair to good, good to great and great to excellent.

The impact of non-school agencies

Policy may be affected by the opinion or vested interests of those who advise government. Official educational policy texts, which include Acts of Parliament and the guidelines produced by government, have an impact on the formulation and public perception of policies (Scott, 2000). OFSTED provides many publications on its website extolling how to be more effective regarding, for example, leadership or the curriculum. Other bodies, such as the National College and professional associations, also commission research into the impact of policy which may influence its future design.

Inconsistency within and between policies

The overt meanings of policy may not be the same as the consequences or outcomes of that policy which can lead to them being at odds with each other (Powell and Edwards, 2005). These can occur because policymakers misunderstand the consequences of the implementation of their policy or suffer from tensions between policies which are working to competing agendas. Examples of non-aligned policies are those regarding standards and inclusion and competition and collaboration. Designing policy may not be straightforward. It can be piecemeal and reactionary and complicated by needing to react to policy that has gone before it. It may be designed by a variety of advisers and organizations, leading to tension, 'fragmentation' and 'unfinished arguments' in its design (Scott, 2000).

The effects of change

The introduction of educational reform is complicated because it is particularly difficult to predict change, as it is not an undifferentiated or linear process (Clarke and Newman 1997). Implementation involves the 'adaptation' of policy by those who implement it (Levin, 2010). Headteachers and others in schools who implement policy must inevitably change it, given the different ways they will interpret its requirements in their own schools. Therefore, it is more likely to be effective if those who are involved have internalized the need for it. This is probably more important in a period of rapid and simultaneous change.

1944–79 A professional partnership: the government, LEAs and the role of the headteacher

There is a degree of popular belief in the existence of the period following the *Education Act* (1944) until the 1970s as being a 'golden age', where headteachers traditionally led in a partnership with LEAs and government in what has been described as a 'national system, locally administered' (Chitty, 2002).

Headteachers were central to the organization of the schools they led. Traditionally, heads set the direction of the school. They were powerful leading professionals managing the development of the curriculum, pedagogy and school organization. In addition, heads often had a teaching role which was considered to be essential in terms of their credibility to parents and to other professionals. Credibility may have been important to heads as a matter of professionalism, however their authority was such that the autonomy of other managers in schools depended largely on their will (Southworth, 2008).

The scope of the decisions headteachers could make at this time was located within fairly narrowly defined parameters. Their accountability was largely defined in terms of that to parents and the LEA, rather than directly to the government. LEAs had some influence on the way headteachers organized the curriculum, as did influential educationalists such as Plowden (1967). Nevertheless, government had a relaxed attitude to the content and means of delivery of the curriculum, which remained in the words of Sir David Eccles, Conservative Minister of Education from 1954–1957 and 1959–1962, 'a secret garden'.

Towards more state intervention

The origins of the movement towards more state control of education can be found in the late 1960s and early 1970s. There was a growing backlash against the perceived failure of progressive education to provide a suitably skilled workforce. Evidence for this can be found in the publication of the Black Papers, which was a series of papers on education edited by Cox and Dyson in the 1960s calling for a return to traditional teaching methods. They were given ammunition by the perceived failure of progressive teaching methods at William Tyndale Junior and Infant School in London.

The origins of the divorce by government from a partnership with the profession can also be traced back to the economic recession where, in the view of Tomlinson (2001), education was being made a 'scapegoat' for economic problems not of their making. Some of the calls for change were ideological. There was a debate about the autonomy of the teaching profession regarding the extent to which they had the right to make decisions about school organization and pedagogy (Kogan, 2002).

A build up of these concerns led to a turning point in the making of educational policy, with a speech by the then Prime Minister James Callaghan at Ruskin College Oxford in 1976. The question was being posed as to whether enough was being done to ensure that school leavers had the required standards of education and skills for employment. Callaghan raised the issue in his speech when he suggested that the education establishment had not yet realized that higher standards were needed in a complex world.

Educational policy 1979–97

From the 1980s, education and the role of the headteacher became framed within a changing political ideology. The acceleration in the movement towards intervention in schools came as a result of a perception mainly held by the business sector and some policy advisers that schools were unresponsive to the needs of the market-driven economy because they were not accountable to the consumer (Walsh, 1994). The autonomy that headteachers had enjoyed as professionals was to change based on a belief that transforming schools from 'domestic' to 'wild' organizations, which have to 'forage for their fodder' (Carlson, 1965, Leithwood et al., 1999, 20) would ensure that only those fit enough would survive in the market. It couldn't be left to chance that the profession would deliver the necessary reforms to education, and so a shift in the attitude of the government towards the profession became manifested in more centralized control and greater accountability.

Successive legislation began a process of holding professionals to account for their performance. *The Education Act* (DES, 1980) strengthened the role of governors and involved them more directly in schools. *The White Paper Better Schools* (DES, 1985a) was not only a discussion of the importance of the role of the headteacher in managing their schools, but also of the contribution which appraisal of the teaching force could make to this. This is a forerunner to the workforce reform legislation of the twenty-first century. These aims were further developed in *Quality in Schools: Education and Appraisal* (DES, 1985b).

One of the strongest measures of control over the profession came in the establishment of the *Teachers Pay and Conditions Act* (DES, 1987), which abolished the negotiating procedures set up in 1965. A reduction of individual teachers' autonomy was accompanied by an increase in the role of headteachers monitoring their schools (Bell, 1999). In the *Teachers Pay and Conditions Act* (DES, 1987), heads were given responsibility for formulating the aims of their schools and monitoring and evaluating the quality and standards of teaching and learning. It was an important development and afterwards dominated the role of headteachers.

It is widely accepted that from its inception, the *Education Reform Act* (ERA) (DES, 1988) dominated education policy and practice. The ERA introduced the prescriptive and then unmanageable national curriculum. This action made it easier to provide for a framework of accountability based on a national system of testing and the production of league tables (Hatcher and Troyna, 1994). The accountability of the profession was strengthened by *The Education (Schools) Act* (DfE, 1992b), which set up OFSTED, which role was monitoring the effectiveness of individual school performances against the requirements of the national policy agenda. However, OFSTED was not without its critics as a framework for accountability. It was considered ineffective by Eric Bolton, the then-Senior Chief Inspector. He argued that it had 'serious shortcomings' and was too 'prescriptive', 'inflexible' and unable to capture the beginning of 'grass roots' problems or developments in schools, and highlighted the independence of the newly created Chief Inspector of Schools (HMCI) as a potential difficulty (Bolton, 1998, 53).

The ERA heralded the beginning of determining the survival of schools through the mechanism of parental choice, which successive governments have adopted. There were flaws in the practice of this argument, as many parents either didn't understand the information given to them in league tables, or, if they did, the schools they chose were often oversubscribed and admission procedure limited entry. Nevertheless, although failing schools didn't close, the idea was an important step on the road to the acceleration of parent power, which has since been an enduring preoccupation of governments.

The declining influence and power of the LEA

The power of local authorities has been weakened. Successive governments have presided over a shift of power from that experienced by Local Education Authorities (LEAs) before the 1980s to schools and other government agencies and quangos (quasi-non-organizational organizations). Local management of schools was introduced in 1988 which delegated school budgets to individual governing bodies and so transferred control of much of government funding from the LEAs directly to schools. This is an enduring feature of the system and one largely welcomed by school leaders. The LEAs' relationship with schools was further eroded with the white paper *Choice and Diversity: A New Framework for Schools* (DfE, 1992a), which allowed schools to apply for grant-maintained status. LEAs no longer had the role of inspection of maintained schools, which was transferred to OFSTED (DfE, 1992b). The DfEE (1996, 48) laid out quite clearly the government's attitude to partnership with LEAs claiming that it wasn't the 'task of LEAs to control or run schools'. They have never recovered from this change in the balance of power between schools and local authorities.

Tensions and dilemmas for headteachers

Government promoted the centrality of headship. This was acknowledged by government agencies with the then HMCI in his Annual Report 1994/1995 viewing the leadership of the headteacher as 'the critical factor in raising standards of pupil achievement' (OFSTED, 1996, 10). In driving its reforms through headteachers, the government created tensions in the role. On the one hand, they were given power to determine budgets, but on the other, their opportunities to make decisions for school improvement were restricted by the creation of the statutory curriculum and OFSTED. Heads had greater independence from the local authority, but at the same time were more accountable to governors for their performance and that of their schools. The work of the headteacher was daunting and intensified by the demands of the pace and change of reform. Increasingly, they needed to fulfil the requirements of the managerial aspects of their role such as financial concerns, as well as to act as the lead professional and curriculum leader in school.

Reforms put a significant burden of accountability on individual headteachers. While being given more autonomy to lead, they were simultaneously more constrained in doing so. Leadership now became located in a framework of a centralized national curriculum and heads had a greater accountability to parents, OFSTED and governors for the performance of the schools they led. Following the reforms offering more parental choice in schooling, it became increasingly important for heads to be successful in marketing their schools as potentially (such as in situations where there were falling roles), they could be working in competition for places due to the formula funded nature of school finances. This caused a dilemma for some who were dismissive of having to market their schools.

New Labour 1997–2001: a new partnership with the profession or more of the same?

There was some excitement felt by members of the profession at the election of New Labour following their promise that 'Education will be our number one priority' (Labour Party, 1997, 5). Many hoped that it would signal the start of a new partnership with the profession. Unfortunately, much of the hope was not to be realized, in the sense that we did not move to a period of trust and autonomy but to one of increased intervention and micromanagement.

Tony Blair was open about continuing some of the policies of the previous government:

> Some things the Conservatives got right. We will not change them. It is where they got things wrong that we will make change. (Labour, 1997, 3)

One of the main changes was to promote a 'third way' for politics, which aimed not only to produce a 'productive economy' but to do so while providing a 'just democracy' (DfEE and QCA, 1999, 10). The dilemma for the government, however, was to ensure a degree of social justice and fairness in its policies while delivering a successful economy.

A commitment to social justice can be identified in Labour's policies. Examples are ensuring the inclusion of children with special needs in mainstream education, and initiatives such as Sure Start, Excellence in Cities, Education Action Zones and possibly in the various schemes to support children in before and after school clubs. The aim was also to encourage innovation from the grass roots in challenging areas with the introduction of the Action Zones, which was an idea from the then-principal adviser to the government, Michael Barber. Unlike the Labour governments of the past, New Labour was happy to embrace a relationship with the private sector such as fostering public private initiatives to build new schools.

Most notably for headteachers, initiatives were accompanied by an increase in interventions into their management of the role. The justification for much of the micro-management heads faced was framed within the concerns of government that the reforms were too important to be left to chance.

The continuation of market ideology and the continuing decline of the power and influence of the LEAs

While individual LEAs may still have played a key role with the profession in their localities, it depended on their capacity and their national role continued to be diminished. The New Labour government enhanced the influence of the private sector with the establishment of City Academies funded directly by the government. Sidelining the LEAs can be seen to have developed even further with the white paper *Schools Achieving Success* (DfES, 2001a). It gave some of its reasoning as the varied quality of LEAs and promoted diversity in the system with the requirement for all new schools to be advertised so that non LEA bodies could apply to manage them.

The relationship between the government and the LEAs also changed as a result of policy regarding target-setting and the plans the LEAs had to produce to respond to the government's agenda for raising standards, complete with a Code of Conduct to ensure the LEA's compliance (DfEE, 1997b; 1998b). As the LEAs were supposed to monitor these targets with schools as well, it changed the relationship it had with headteachers and became, in this way at least, more challenging.

Standards and accountability

Much of the improvement to the education system was to be delivered by concentrating on 'standards' and this impacted particularly on the role of the primary headteacher. An example of New Labour's commitment to standards was its creation of the Standards and Effectiveness Unit in 1997. Its remit was to work in partnership with schools and LEAs and others committed to developing and implementing the government's various strategies to raise standards.

The government was to be relentless in its pursuit of high standards of pupil achievement. The white paper *Excellence in Schools* (DfEE, 1997a) called for the elimination of underachievement and the overcoming of social disadvantage with the intention of strengthening accountability. The position of the headteacher in the government's reforms was reinforced by the same white paper, where it opined that 'Good heads can transform a school; poor heads can block progress or achievement.' (p. 46) By the time the green paper *Schools Building on Success: Raising Standards* (DfES, 2001b) was published, the government was able to report on the improvement of literacy and numeracy. This was measured by the end of KS2 standardized assessment tests (SATs), with 75 per cent of children achieving L4 and above in English, compared to 57 per cent in 1996 and 72 per cent in maths in 2000, compared with 54 per cent in 1996.

Although the standards initially improved due to the 'success' of the National Strategies and the 'training program' which accompanied them (Barber, 2002, 182), they plateaued during Labour's second term. KS2 results for English remained static at 75 per cent for three years. In 2002, the government failed to reach its original literacy and numeracy targets at the end of KS2, that 80 per cent of children in English and 75 per cent of children in maths would reach L4+. The response to schools' failure to achieve the targets set by the government was to extend the time for attaining them to 2004, but at the same time it was acknowledged that the system had perhaps run out of steam and needed to change.

The call for system redesign

It was generally accepted that, approximately coinciding with the second term of the Labour government, the system was becoming inadequate to manage the current and future pressures placed upon it. These were identified as the need to educate for a knowledge economy, the impact of succession management due to the impending retirement of the 'baby boomer' generation, and the plateauing standards at the end of KS2 tests from 2000.

A recognition of the importance of effective school leadership to the needs of the economy produced managerialism and a form of compliance by schools and 'designer leadership' of headteachers in order that the government could manage their role within the system (Gronn, 2003). Managerialism has dominated the school system through the setting of targets for performance and the measurement of them by the government through its accountability systems. These have evaluated individual schools through the monitoring of performance of headteachers and their teams. The aim was to 'create an error-free' and 'risk-less organisation' in which professionals don't need to be trusted because the system is so carefully controlled and micro-managed (Bottery, 2004, 25).

The effects of managerialism increased bureaucracy and so the aims of the private sector to create a lean and fit organization which can move faster in a global and fast-changing world hadn't transpired (Farrell and Morris, 2003). The system needed to change in order to provide leadership which is both effective and knowledgeable enough to respond to complex and rapid change (Bentley, 2003). The policy of micro-management of the profession delivered through targets only strengthened managerialism and was considered to be no longer effective on its own. Consequently, the system needed to be redesigned through government policy which necessitated changes to the role of headteacher and created new patterns of school leadership.

The 'mess' of system redesign

One of the difficulties for the education system lies in the nature of the problems and issues it is trying to solve. They have been described using Heifetz's (1994) term as a 'complex adaptive challenge', because previous or known technical solutions are no longer appropriate. They are also a 'mess' (Ackoff, 1974). Chapman (2002) describes the differences between a 'mess' and a 'difficulty'. They are complementary terms and shouldn't be seen as being in competition with each other. Difficulties are problems which have general agreement on what the problem is and what some or part of the solution would look like. Chapman (2002) sees them as '*bounded*' (original emphasis) by time and resources needed to resolve them. Messes however are unbounded with no clear agreement as to what the problem is and uncertainty or ambiguity in how to resolve them. Change is difficult to predict and 'non linear' (Clarke and Newman, 1997). Therefore instead of a single solution to a single problem or incremental change successful system change entails thinking about whole and interrelated systems.

In the light of this, it is important to consider how the main policies which impact on the current agendas of headteachers manifest whole system change or small piecemeal fragments. In doing so, there is less likelihood of tensions in policymaking caused between competing issues or poor linkage of policies. Examples of these are competition for school places between schools on one hand and collaborative working between them on the other or the need to raise standards within a framework of inclusion.

That these conditions haven't been in place can be identified by a sharp increase in the creation of policies by the government as it tries to mitigate the impact of the implementation of its existing policies. Previous policies can have failed in their intention, or have had unintended consequences. When these haven't worked, they have required yet more policies to correct. Policy modification and often the components of the policies themselves have been described as 'inevitably a process of bricolage' and 'compromise' (Ball 1998, 126), and more of what can be done than should be done (Levin, 2003).

Unintended consequences can cause a failure in educational policy, because innovation is transformed by those involved in the process (Clarke and Newman, 1997). How headteachers and others will react to policy is difficult to predict and may be contradictory. Reaction can be complicated if headteachers are trying to overcome the negative effects of poorly designed policy in different ways according to their own context.

As organizations adapt slowly, March and Olsen (1989) maintain that change is therefore best developed over time. Managerialism however tends towards short-term solutions, such as the Literacy and Numeracy Strategies, because performance management and other forms of measurement such as the SATs results and league tables are short-term goals. Organizations may also have to adapt quickly if they have subsequently been seen to fail, and headteachers have to impose change designed for school improvement to which the school has to adapt quickly. Direct intervention, or centrally imposed policy reform which controls what happens, is considered by Bentley (2002) as being unsuitable for the complexities of the education system. Micro-managing the implementation of educational policy doesn't allow for innovation and change by schools. For change to work it is important that the need for it is recognised and supported by those who implement it.

What needed to change?

Fullan (2005) was concerned that externally imposed vision can limit the scope of school improvement approaches, which could otherwise develop but would be constrained due to a 'contrived coherence'. Any improvements made will be put at risk by over prescription and centralisation of education. So, while headteachers may have learnt to adapt, school improvements were being constrained by the micro-management of government policy and initiatives.

There was also a complication caused by a shortage of school leaders and a real concern identified by commentators that there would be a shortage of headteachers from 2009 to 2014, with nearly half of them eligible for retirement. While the consequences of the retirement of the 'baby boomer' generation may have required system change in themselves, another issue for concern was the identification of a growing disengagement of leaders with a 'reluctance' on the part of senior managers to become leaders. Finding solutions to these problems had to be planned for in schools. Preparing LAs and schools to manage succession became one of the principal goals of the National College (NCSL, 2006).

Many headteachers felt that their actions were constrained due to the many government-imposed initiatives, OFSTED, league tables and the public shame of failure. This was not a conducive climate to taking risks and acting courageously in the best interests of raising standards of achievement. While many school leaders were indeed 'courageous' in their actions, they may also have had a strong sense of self-preservation for themselves and their schools and so may have been reluctant to prioritise for the best and instead taking the least risky solution.

There was a growing recognition by government that there was a degree of autonomy needed for school leaders to deal with the policy 'mess' at their level and that the necessary degree of autonomy was not available in the system to enable them to do so. In which case, a different relationship between the government and school leadership had to be built up through an 'earned autonomy' (Morris, 2001). There also needed to be some understanding of what the required change was to look like and if individual schools were to be allowed to work independently there was the danger of the kind of piecemeal or fragmented approach to system change outlined earlier and so therefore this argument required the innovation to be at system level.

The Challenges of Headship: Policies and Themes from Labour's Second Term and the Coalition

2

As the system transforms, there are fundamental changes taking place for primary headteachers in their role and relationships with others. Solving these issues during the last decade has led to changing patterns of school leadership within the school system, in terms of roles both inside and outside school. I recognize that the issues and themes I have chosen to consider regarding their impact on school leaders is not exhaustive. They have been chosen because they represent the key policy changes which relate to those areas identified by headteachers as impacting on their role. They are:

- Workforce reform: managing performance and changing staffing structures
- Standards and the curriculum
- Accountability

- Social justice as a driver of change
- Changing patterns of school leadership

Workforce reform: managing performance and changing staffing structures

The last decade has seen significant changes made to reform the workforce. Despite early interventions in the 1990s by government to manage performance, the strategies they used weren't entirely successful. From experience, I am aware that the use of appraisal by the end of the 1990s was mostly unregulated. This situation began to change with the publication of the green paper *Teachers Meeting the Challenge of Change* (DfEE, 1998a). One of its aims was to modernize the teaching profession using two main policies, which were changes to the appraisal framework and remodelling the workforce.

From 2000, a new pay system through performance management and threshold and post-threshold scales was the mechanism by which the government's strategy for appraisal and beginning to remodel the workforce was implemented. The government required some degree of quality assurance of the process and created a system of external assessors to verify the judgements of headteachers. Not all agree with the merits of performance management, and Ball (2003) argues that a rigorous form of appraisal meant that the worth of the profession was being determined by performance comparisons artificially and inaccurately determined.

By 2003, the government's emphasis had moved from performance management to concentrate on remodelling the workforce (Rutherford, 2004), which was part of the government's strategy to raise standards and to support the aims of the 1998 green paper. Earlier reforms were complemented by the workforce reform legislation in the form of *The National Agreement on Raising Standards and Tackling Workload: A National Agreement* (DfES, 2003c). This was designed to raise standards, while at the same time tackle what was being acknowledged (Price Waterhouse Coopers, 2001) as an unmanageable workload for teachers and headteachers and one which threatened a crisis in recruitment and retention in the profession.

The implementation of workforce reform legislation was a slow process because it was often challenged by the employee associations, with the agreement of the Workforce Agreement Monitoring Group (WAMG) being a necessary part of the reform process. The reforms for tackling workload were implemented between 2003 and 2005 and included the removal of administrative tasks for teachers (2003), changes to cover arrangements for teachers with the use of support staff (2004), and in 2005 the operation of time for planning, preparation and assessment (PPA). The latter also included dedicated time for headship, as part of the strategy for the retention of heads. However, it missed the point that heads are accountable for their role and required to complete tasks, irrespective of dedicated headship time. So while it may have legitimized time headteachers take to reflect on school improvement issues, it didn't alleviate the problems of work intensification.

One way of overcoming the workload of headteachers is to lead more strategically (Price Waterhouse Coopers, 2007). If heads are to lead more strategically, more of their role must be distributed to others in school, and workforce reform can be used to accomplish this. The reforms contained in *The National Agreement* (DfES, 2003c) led to increased responsibilities in school for support staffs. One example of improving workload for headteachers has been the growth of the role of school business manager. Changes to the role of non-teaching staff also facilitated the opportunity for schools to become multi-agency organizations and, as such, a fundamental part of the extended schools reform of the Labour government.

Performance management as a tool for tackling underperformance was seen by the Coalition government to be too slow to be effective. The government intended to rectify this by pledging to 'remove the current duplication between the performance management and the "capability" procedures for managing poor performance' (DfE, 2010b, 25).

Standards and the curriculum

The National Curriculum, testing and assessment had long been used by government to produce a benchmark against which parents could judge schools. The Labour government, however, increased the intensity of the drive for standards in schools through its use of targets, evident in the publication of detailed guidance on target setting for literacy and numeracy (DfEE, 1997b). The relentless pursuit of higher standards continued with the introduction of the *Standards and Framework Act* (DfEE, 1998b). It retained much of previous Conservative policy regarding the standards agenda (i.e. league tables, testing, national curriculum and local management of schools).

The Literacy (DfEE, 1998c) and Numeracy (1998d) Strategies were introduced into schools in September 1998 and 1999, respectively. They were a measure designed to reduce variability between schools by prescribing both what was taught and, more controversially, how to teach it. They were variously welcomed by teachers as a useful guide as to what to do or as an unwelcome intrusion into their professionalism. In 2000, following the Qualifications and Curriculum Authority (QCA) Curriculum Review, headteachers were able to cut back on time given to music, PE and art to give more time to literacy and numeracy. Any criticism that this may have led to a shortage of time given to other subjects was second to the real pressure from government at this time for headteachers to improve standards in literacy and numeracy.

Standards rose initially. However, this may have been at least partly due to hot-housing children's learning due to the increased time given to them rather than any innate quality of the National Strategies themselves. There has been some sensitivity on behalf of government agencies regarding the imposition of the strategies. This has included suggestions that, in respect of the numeracy strategy at least, heads lacked understanding of how it could be used for school improvement and had followed the strategies without enough questioning (OFSTED, 2002a; 2002b). As a practising headteacher at the time, I concur with Bottery's (2007) views and confirm that it was known the strategies were not statutory but the crucial factor is that they were heavily supported by LEAs, and OFSTED expected headteachers to report on them.

There was growing recognition at this time that the system was at a tipping point and standards must be raised (Barber, 2005). Being overly explicit in the management of headteachers through a command and control approach to the curriculum was no longer working to produce the creativity and innovation needed in a knowledge economy (Hartley, 2003). The launch of *Excellence and Enjoyment: A Strategy for Primary Schools* (DfES, 2003b) was designed to offer some flexibility and innovation in the curriculum. It brought with it at least some acknowledgement of the value of enjoyment in children's learning, although it was a false dawn for radical change.

A further attempt to reduce centralization and respond to the need to offer flexibility and a more contextually based approach to the curriculum lies in the call to personalize learning. The government was careful to explain that this was not to be assumed by the profession to be a return to 'child-centred theories' (Miliband, 2004), possibly harking back to earlier criticism of progressive education. However, despite aims to reduce its top-down approach towards the curriculum and its assessment by government, headteachers were left in no doubt as to the importance of standards. They were still being held to account for the performance of their schools through the imposition of targets monitored by OFSTED. This was not a conducive climate towards risk taking and innovation.

The Children's Plan (DCSF, 2007) called for a review of the national curriculum, which was to be fundamental and to have the flexibility to personalize learning. In January 2008, Sir Jim Rose was commissioned by Ed Balls, the then-Secretary of State for Education, to undertake this review and his final report was published in April 2009. The Rose Curriculum Review concentrated on what should be taught and pedagogy. Targets and testing were deliberately left out of its remit. It underwent an extensive consultation process with the profession, parents and the QCA. However, by the time schools were about to implement its recommendations, it was shelved by the incoming Coalition government. Their intention was to create a new curriculum because:

> at present, the National Curriculum includes too much that is not essential knowledge, and there is too much prescription about how to teach. (DfE, 2010b, 10)

The new curriculum was to focus on 'core knowledge in the traditional subject disciplines' (DfE, 2010b, 42), to be gained in each key stage, rather than the skill-based curriculum suggested by the Rose Review. In prescribing core knowledge, it is clear that the government was prepared to be interventionist, despite any rhetoric to the contrary. Further evidence of this is also illustrated by the government's expectation for every school to teach a system of synthetic phonics. They perceived this as the most suitable method for teaching reading, which they were prepared to reinforce through the expectation that OFSTED inspectors and trainee teachers be given the wherewithal to assess and teach it, respectively (DfE, 2010b).

Accountability

There are different forms of professional accountability to which headteachers need to respond, such as accountability to parents, staff and themselves as professionals. However, the major form of accountability for headteachers in the English system is being accountable through the mechanism of OFSTED for the performance of their schools. One reason given to endorse the use of OFSTED was that inspections contribute to raising standards in schools

(Woodhead, 1999). However, as standards plateaued from 2000, this was no longer a realistic argument and the rhetoric of government began to change. From this juncture, the government began to emphasize its understanding of the bureaucratic workload of teachers.

It began to discuss the need for self-evaluation and shorter inspections, known as 'light touch', for schools deemed to be effective. Whether this was more of a recognition that the system wasn't working to deliver improved standards rather than a genuine concern over the bureaucratic workload of teachers is debatable. However, Tomlinson, the then-HMCI, was careful to note that self-evaluation wouldn't lead to a lack of 'rigour' in school inspections (Learner, 2001). This view highlighted a dilemma for those in government. Advisors close to government were recognizing the need to allow a degree of 'informed professionalism' (Barber, 2002), but at the same time didn't want to open the way for a 'thousand flowers to bloom' and lose control of the system. Therefore, calls came for a more 'intelligent' form of accountability which balanced external and internal accountability.

The New Relationship with Schools (DfES/OFSTED, 2004) was introduced as a solution to some of the problems outlined above. Improvements were to be achieved through a combination of schools self-assessment by producing a report on an online self-evaluation form (SEF) and external assessment working together. A 'single conversation' with a school improvement partner (SIP) was also the basis of this new relationship working in partnership with schools towards school improvement (Hopkins, 2005).

Although not described as such by the government, the role of SIP could also be seen to be part of a solution to solve any dips in performance not picked up between inspections masked in the user-friendly terms of a critical friendship. This would enable a degree of confidence on the part of the government that schools were being monitored if inspections became less frequent.

The theme of less bureaucracy and compliance was a feature of the rhetoric of the Coalition government. This intention is a thread running through the white paper *The Importance of Teaching* (DfE, 2010b). In it, government purported to be willing to reduce centralized control, and one response to this was to abolish the requirement to respond to centrally driven target setting, the role of the SIP in schools and the expectation that each school would fill in a SEF submitted online.

Earned autonomy was a feature of the Labour government's policy, but the micro-management of school leaders came in the force of directives

and guidelines. The framework for OFSTED current in 2010 had 27 different headings for judgements. The Coalition identified changes it intended to
make to reduce the schedule for inspection to four main areas: pupil achievement, the quality of teaching, leadership and management, and the behaviour and safety of pupils. Those who had gained validation through good and
better inspection grades were to be given a greater degree of autonomy, and
outstanding schools were to be released from routine inspections. However,
those schools which were considered vulnerable were to be subjected to
greater intervention (DfE, 2010b).

Data

The aim of the Labour government to reduce workload was unsuccessful and
it was increased by the requirement for headteachers to gather data as evidence of their school's performance for the SEF to inform inspection judgements. An industry formed around companies advising schools as to what
to keep and the best ways of keeping it. Miliband (2004) identified data as
'the most valuable currency in school improvement'. Unfortunately, there
have been concerns expressed as to the validity of the data collected (Gorard,
2006), leading to a potential lack of accuracy in judging a school's performance and the impact on the workload of headteachers in gathering it.

Apart from the inadequacies in the marking processs, which came to the
attention of the media in the SATs debacle of 2008, there was also the issue
that to hold schools accountable for attainment irrespective of context was
unfair. The Labour government sought to offset this problem by introducing contextual value added (CVA) data to use to judge schools' performance.
This was expected to go some way to iron out the disadvantages of some contexts. However, to do so necessitates the accurate gathering and interpreting
of data and that it is used as a guide rather than as the main determinant of
an inspection outcome. The issues surrounding the inaccurate and negative
use of data highlighted in the Times Educational Supplement (TES) (Stewart,
2009) suggested that the aims of intelligent accountability to create the conditions for professional autonomy and fair accountability and, therefore, system
development had not been realized.

The House of Commons Select Committee published a critical report
(House of Commons, 2008) about the value of high-stakes testing in determining the performance of primary children and the effectiveness of their
schools. This was confirmed through evidence submitted to the Cambridge

Primary Review set up by the Esme Fairbairn Foundation to review primary education, which reported in 2009.

In 2010, the issues around the unfairness of testing came to a head when the National Association for Headteachers (NAHT) balloted its members with a view to boycotting the administration of Key Stage 2 (KS2) SATs. Many did so, prompting a quick response to the issue by the incoming Coalition government. The SATs for 7 and 11 year olds were to remain but there was an agreement to:

> hold an independent review of key stage two testing, seeking to retain a strong basis for accountability and information to parents and secondary schools, while alleviating the damaging effects of over-rehearsal of tests. (DfE, 2010b, 11)

This agreement and forthcoming review by Lord Bew forestalled any action likely to be taken by headteachers in boycotting SATs. The government also signalled its intention to introduce new tests with the introduction of a reading test for 6 year olds and again at 11 years old to assess children's ability to decode words. The white paper (DfE, 2010b) announced that a new testing agency was to be set up to review tests and assessments for pupils up to age 14. The abolition of the Qualifications and Curriculum Development Agency (QCDA) meant that its role and work were transferred to the Secretary of State.

Plateauing standards had been the reason behind much of the policy of the Labour government. However, performance at the end of Key Stage 2 measured by pupils achieving Level 4 and above was also plateauing in 2010. The results were 80 per cent English and 79 per cent Maths, and the DfE site noted that in comparison overall to the revised 2009 statistics, 'Achievement has remained the same in English and mathematics' (DfE and BIS, 2010). The Coalition introduced a new 'floor standard' of attainment, concerned with the number of pupils achieving below L4, together with a measurement of how well pupils from disadvantaged backgrounds attained in tests.

However, while acknowledging value added in terms of pupil progress made in levels, this was not to include a measurement for context (DfE, 2010b). The Coalition argued that CVA had been discredited as a measurement for pupil progress. It highlighted CVA as both difficult for parents to understand and not as reliable a predictor of future success as attainment scores. They took an opposite view to that of the Labour government and were not prepared to consider context as part of the measurement of progress. The Coalition believed CVA allowed for excuses to be made for a poorer performance from certain groups of pupils, and so signalled it would abolish the measurement in the white paper (DfE, 2010b).

Social justice as a driver of change

There was concern from the Labour government that, despite some improvement in standards, there were not sufficient improvements made by those children who were from disadvantaged backgrounds. This was despite Education Action Zones meant to address this issue. Policies introduced from the second term of the Labour government reflect its aims to raise standards of performance and children's well-being using a whole systems approach to integrating education and children's services. Labour's commitment to early provision to ensure a minimizing of social deprivation is to be found in the Sure Start scheme set up in 1997 and was the first phase of 'joined up' multi-agency services.

Sure Start was to be further developed in the green paper *Every Child Matters* (2003a), followed by *The Children's Act* (DfES, 2004a), which ensured the '5 Outcomes' of safety, health, enjoying and achieving, economic awareness and making a positive contribution were embedded into schools' provision. It also led to the introduction of children's centres developed from the Sure Start initiative as a support to families for childcare, family support and employment help through Job Centre Plus. Many were located on school sites, with implications for changing the role of the headteacher.

It had been possible since *The Education Act* (2002) for governing bodies to provide extended services for the benefit of the children in their schools or locality for charitable purposes. The DfES (2005a) introduced a prospectus detailing its expectations regarding extended schools provision. It outlined the expectation that by 2010, wrap-around childcare would be offered from 8 am before school to 6 pm after school. This could be provided by a number of sources, to include schools and private agencies working on or off school premises. The publication of *The Children's Plan* (DCSF, 2007), which set out the government's goals until 2020, clearly indicated that the continued moves towards extended services and the continuance of an inclusive approach to child care and education was to be driven through school leadership.

From September 2009, OFSTED had to report on the care of children in the Early Years Foundation Stage (EYFS), and from 2010, it inspected the children's centres located on schools sites. The Labour government continued to champion wider partnerships in education. One of these was to ensure that schools continued to work towards the Every Child Matters (ECM) agenda. To assist, they intended to 'support the creation of multi-agency teams in schools and bring schools and wider services together in Children's Trusts' (DCSF, 2009, 43). To help to secure the delivery of its agenda, the government made training for Directors of Children's Services (DCS) part of the remit of the National College (NC, 2009a), necessitating its change of name.

The Coalition changed the national policy approach to multiple agencies and the role of the local authority was reduced with respect to children's services agenda. Thus, the Coalition viewed education policy as 'substantially school's policy', which was 'exemplified' in the change of name from DCSF to DfE (Husbands, 2011). The government was still committed to raising standards for all and introduced a pupil premium to be paid to schools for each of their economically disadvantaged pupils entitled to free school meals (DfE, 2010b). However, in keeping with their wish to allow freedom to heads at local level, this wasn't ring-fenced funding, and how the money was allocated was left to the individual school. The potential consequences of this, especially with reducing school budgets, is that the money will be used as part of school's general budgets and not specifically for disadvantaged pupils.

The Coalition was keen to reduce the prescription and unnecessary interventions it perceived as accompanying the ECM agenda introduced by Labour. They promised to reduce bureaucracy and empower school leaders, who they believed understood how to support their communities without statutory requirements. The government announced therefore an intention to remove the duty for schools to co-operate with Children's Trusts (DfE, 2010b) Community cohesion, possibly regarded by Labour as a way of forcing its agenda through schools, was to be removed from the OFSTED framework. The government's intention was to rely on schools working together and with voluntary organizations to provide a range of extended school services.

Changing patterns of school leadership

New forms of school leadership of single institutions have developed. This includes shared headship and headship involving multi-agency partnerships, such as children's centres; co-locations of different settings, such as special schools and mainstream schools on one site; and all through 0–19 provision all of which impact on the leadership *capacity* of the headteacher to manage them (Southworth, 2008, original emphasis).

A particular feature of New Labour policy was to improve education by encouraging collaboration between schools. This policy led to changes to the role of the headteacher in their being used to solve system-wide issues such as succession management and spreading effective practice, particularly through school-to-school support for those in challenging circumstances and vulnerable to failure through inspection. The use of schools in leading change was judged necessary as the 'top down' centralized one-size-fits all-approach was inflexible and ineffective (Chapman, 2002).

An early indication of government's intention can be seen in the white paper *Schools Achieving Success* (DfES, 2001a, 6), where 'well led' schools were to be able to 'take full responsibility for their mission', thus suggesting a degree of earned autonomy, and later the suggestion that the 'best schools' will be used to 'lead the system' (DfES, 2001a, 37). This view presupposes that OFSTED is the best mechanism to determine the effectiveness of schools. As outcomes are so predetermined by data attached to performance, this may not be an effective way for primary schools of determining autonomy. Nevertheless, a number of school leaders who could act as 'practitioner champions' (Hargreaves, 2003) and lead innovation successfully outside their school were identified as 'system leaders' (Fullan, 2005). They were created to build capacity in the system, which required new ways of working by government to facilitate, and by school leaders to be motivated to lead with moral purpose (Hopkins, 2006).

The use of system leaders is pragmatic as it offers a solution to the twin dilemmas of distributing effective practice and extending the leadership of headteachers across more than one school to manage succession. System leaders can be identified as having the 'informed professionalism' advocated by Barber and Fullan (2005). The extent to which this was freedom only for those who are informed in the right way about the required areas has led to some criticism of headteachers who implement government policy acting as 'policy entrepreneurs' (Kingdon, 2003, in Gunter, 2008).

The role of consultant leader was recognised by the DfES in the role of Primary Strategy Consultant Leader (PSCL) and consultant leadership through the London Challenge (DfES, 2003e). This was originally established by the government to improve underperforming secondary schools in London, extended to primary schools from 2008 and developed the use of school leaders working to support each other as a leadership strategy. PSCLs were introduced through the Primary Leadership Programme (PLP) (DfES, 2003d), which was launched as part of the Primary National Strategy, with training programmes provided by the NCSL through LAs for heads to act as consultants in schools deemed as vulnerable. There was an expectation by government that such vulnerability would distinguish itself through low results and, hence, these schools would be targeted.

The training and brokerage for such a programme came via the local authorities, which meant that they had a high degree of opportunity to shape the programme and placement of consultants according to local need. The variable quality and capacity of LAs will also have impacted on the effectiveness of the initiative in each locality. Nevertheless, a study carried out into the effectiveness of the PLP identified that the early use of system leaders had achieved some success. There was a higher improvement in English and mathematics scores in those schools in the programme than in those schools used for comparison not in the PLP (Wade et al., 2007).

Interest in the use of system leaders to improve schools continued, and in 2005, the DfES identified a role for school leaders:

> who have the talent and experience . . . [and] with the ability to run our most challenging schools. (DfES, 2005b, 100)

They would be encouraged to work outside their own school, collaborating with others. In order to facilitate this, the government in the same white paper proposed that NCSL working with the National Strategies would train and develop leaders of 'complex schools' and 'federations', and it became part of their remit letter following the end-to-end review (DfES, 2004b). NCSL (2005) pledged its support to developing NLEs and to ensuring they were placed in the most complex and challenging schools. The NLE initiative was evaluated as effective in raising standards of attainment and in other aspects of a schools performance in the supported schools (Hill and Matthews, 2008). The National College continued to promote school-to-school support:

> To develop world-class school leadership, we need to encourage the best school leaders to support the rest – both within and across schools. (NC, 2009b, 106)

In 2010, Hill and Matthews evaluated the impact of NLEs for a second time and identified that NLEs and their schools were 'making a significant contribution to supporting improvement in under-performing schools' (2010, 13). However, the 'full potential' of the role had 'still yet to be realised' (18). Local Leaders of Education (LLE) were also introduced into the system as school to school support. They are successful heads who are expected to provide 'coaching and mentoring support to headteachers of schools facing challenges' (NC, 2009b, 31). The main difference between LLEs and NLEs is that they are not expected to use a support team from their own school while acting as consultant headteachers.

The power to intervene in schools in difficulty was delegated to LAs, and they were expected to identify schools in weakness through their own monitoring or using OFSTED's judgement. Subsequent improvement strategies were at the discretion of the LA and, despite powers granted to it by *The Education Act* (2002) and firmed up in *The Education and Inspections Act* (2006), only in extreme circumstances would the government intervene to close a school. The 2006 Education Act stated that LAs could also force schools that were in a failing OFSTED category to enter into collaboration with another successful school. A hardening attitude can be detected in the white paper *Your Child, Your Schools, Our Future: Building a 21st-Century Schools System* (DCSF, 2009). It strengthened the powers of LAs to intervene in failing or coasting schools using outstanding schools as support. If the LA didn't do so, the power of the Secretary of State was to be extended to intervene directly. The government's commitment to using headteachers was clear:

> federation and other partnership solutions will become central to tackling weakness and extending the reach of the best leaders. (DCSF, 2009, 44)

One form of partnership introduced in the same white paper was for the use of Accredited Providers or Groups. They were to lead the system by tackling underperformance and effect lasting change in vulnerable schools.

The period of the second and third terms of the Labour government saw a dramatic rise in partnerships between schools. While acknowledging the role of business partnerships in school, perhaps the key player for primary school partnerships at this time was the National College – due to their role with the introduction and leadership of the Networked Learning Communities initiative. Other networks were formed as a result of the extended schools cluster work, and it was anticipated by the Labour government that schools would work with newly formed school trusts (DCSF, 2009). This was a short lived policy as the Coalition signalled its intention to remove the obligation for schools to work with school trusts (DfE, 2010b).

In considering system leadership, some of the main partnerships and networks for headteachers were formed for supporting vulnerable schools. The main benefits of such partnership working were identified by Hargreaves (2010, 6–7). Some of these were being more able to accommodate the needs of pupils and staff by sharing the capacity of more than one school by working together, to distribute 'knowledge' and 'innovation' within the group and from those external agencies with which they work, an efficient use of resources and to 'protect' those in the group who might be 'vulnerable to crisis and failure'.

Following the election of the Coalition government in May 2010, there was a continuity of approach to school collaboration for improvement:

> We expect schools to use their increased autonomy to explore new ways of working together – but collaboration in the future will be driven by school leaders and teachers – not bureaucrats. (DfE, 2010b, 52)

The key difference in approach between the two governments was that centralization was a feature of the Labour government in its attempts to drive forward school improvement initiatives. The rhetoric from its second term of office was towards a more balanced approach between centralization and autonomy of action for the profession with its use of system leaders and latterly Accredited School Groups (DCSF, 2009). This move indicated an increasing realization by Labour that schools working together to improve the system achieve better results for overall system improvement than do initiatives driven purely from the centre, as they can solve the issues at ground level. The Coalition accelerated the process of driving school improvement locally through clusters and networks of schools. They facilitated this approach through the speedy introduction of school structural reform (see next section).

The NLE and LLE roles already well established were central to this drive for school collaboration and improvement at local level and their numbers were to be increased. In addition, Specialist Leaders of Education (SLEs) who are professionals other than headteachers was a role introduced in the white paper (DfE, 2010b). It was recognized that there were excellent professionals in many schools, including those schools deemed by OFSTED to be failing in some ways. Within these schools, too, there would be areas of excellent practice and staff at different levels, such as middle leaders and SBMs who needed to be encouraged to work with those in similar positions in other schools. Unless they were in National Support Schools or other good schools, and their head was engaged in school improvement work, they might not otherwise be given the opportunity to do so.

Changing school structures and organization

The Labour government encouraged the concept of federations of two or more schools from its second term and introduced legislation to support it. *The Education Act* (2002) defined a federation as having:

> a single governing body constituted under a single instrument of government. (DfES, 2002, section 24)

Technically, according to this definition, all other arrangements with more than one governing body were forms of collaboration. However, at the time there was a wide use of the term 'federation'. It became applied quite 'loosely' and used to include school amalgamations and 'hard' and 'soft' federations (Southworth, 2008) which were dependent on the role of the governing body. The range was identified as a 'Collaborative Federation Continuum' (DfES and The Innovations Unit 2005, 6). These organizations varied from collaborations with no joint governance to soft federations with one or more joint governors' committees, followed by more formal or fixed joint governance, and finally a hard federation with a single governing body. Only what used to be termed 'hard federations; are genuine federations, and all other arrangements are collaborations.

The composition of groups of schools varies. Business and charity sponsorship of academies was a feature of groups of secondary or cross-phase federations or collaborations under the Labour government. Other examples are single secondary or primary phase, cross phase with primary and secondary or middle and upper schools, and all through 3–19 schools. Sometimes, collaboration was manifested in forming a trust of successful schools in a locality. Trusts were either single schools or groups of two or more. Trust partners included business sponsors: universities, other schools (often included to support in a performance trust) and the LA. These schools could be involved as a federation. In this case, there may have been more than one headteacher in the group.

Many federations or collaborations were formed as a school improvement measure when a school was failing (DCSF, 2009). They were often the result of school-to-school improvement, frequently via NLE involvement. While there may be an expectation that federations and chains work to support other schools, there was no proviso that they do so. In addition, federations were used to solve the issue of leadership succession in small schools which otherwise found it difficult to recruit. In these circumstances, there would be one headteacher across a number of schools. Staffs were often deployed across the schools but budgets were delegated to each school, dictated by its pupil numbers. Very often, schools in federations retained their own distinctive identity. However, there was a growing phenomenon of chains of schools, particularly in the secondary phase, which were more likely to operate as a brand, with operating systems common to all in the chain (Hill, 2010).

Groups of schools were subject to separate inspections for each school. There were difficulties for headteachers of potentially having several inspections in quick succession if they led several schools. Leadership was also judged separately. The Labour government, possibly recognizing these difficulties, identified the need for schools to be judged in relation to the quality of their work in partnership. This could relate to any form of collaboration. They further indicated that OFSTED was to introduce a revised grade for partnership work and would carry out more inspections of federations (DCSF, 2009).

The white paper (DCSF, 2009) introduced accreditation for outstanding schools. This gave either individual schools or school groups, sometimes including those led by business, faith groups or charity sponsors, the opportunity to gain the Accredited Schools quality mark, which enabled them to run chains of schools. To qualify, heads had to prove successful leadership in supporting other schools in challenging circumstances and to have effected improvement. The system initially for secondary schools was to be extended to include primary schools to be accredited in March 2010. Although a first round of schools was accredited, some of which are represented in this study, the Coalition government discontinued the initiative.

The Coalition government: increasing school diversity

To increase school-to-school collaboration, the Coalition signalled its intention to encourage more groups of outstanding primary leaders and sponsors, of schools. Examples of company sponsors include ARK Schools an educational charity or the Harris Academies set up by Lord Harris Chairman and Chief Executive of Carpetright plc to undertake the leadership of federations and chains to drive the 'improvement of the whole school system' (DfE, 2010b, 57). In doing so, they were to build on the existing system of school partnerships developed as part of Labour education policy. In addition, they wished to create further autonomy through new school organizations believing it would have a 'galvanising' effect to introduce new state-funded schools. It alluded in the white paper (DfE, 2010b) to a 'curtailment' of 'freedom to innovate', despite the introduction by Labour of academies and city technology colleges. In making its case, the Coalition highlighted the PISA data from 'the highest performing school jurisdictions' and naming some of these as U.S. charter schools, Alberta, Canada and Swedish Free Schools. The white paper argued for a greater number of similar independent state schools in England.

Academies

One of the first pieces of major legislation enacted by the Coalition was the *Academies Act*, which was in force by the end of July (DfE, 2010a) in time for new academies to open in September 2010. Such haste illustrates the speed at which the government intended to pursue its education reforms. The new academies differed from those of the previous government. Labour had used sponsorship from charities and businesses to fund the conversion of failing secondary schools to academies. After these were seen to achieve some success, there was an increase in the sponsorship of more than one academy under the same sponsor, such as the ARK or Harris groups. Some academies were all through schools and so included the primary age range, but there were no purely primary phase academies. This was to change under the Coalition:

> It is our ambition that Academy status should be the norm for all state schools, with schools enjoying direct funding and full independence from central and local bureaucracy. (DfE, 2010b, 52)

Outstanding schools could automatically convert from September 2010. While the government hailed the expression of interest from 22 per cent of outstanding primary schools, it must be remembered that pressing a button on the DfE website to find out more information is not the same as wishing to convert. From November 2010, schools judged good with outstanding features were also invited to apply and from early 2011 it was announced that all schools would be considered.

Another key difference between the Labour and Coalition academies was that the support of the LA was required for the former, which also had a role in governance. The changes meant that some schools made the decision to convert in the face of LA opposition. The opportunity to convert to academy status was also compatible with the government's rhetoric of granting autonomy to the best school leaders. The introduction of Coalition Academies would, according to the government, allow these schools to shape their own ethos and framework free from bureaucratic control. Therefore, they were meant to complement the existing academy programme rather than replace it. While being freed from LA bureaucracy in how they were led and the need to follow the national curriculum, academies would still be subject to assessment of their performance. All state-funded schools were to be held accountable in tests which would reflect the national curriculum (DfE, 2010b).

Free schools

Under the *Academies Act* (2010a), the Coalition government offered opportunities for teachers' groups, charities, faith groups and parents to open new state-funded independent schools, known as free schools. These are an example of policy borrowing in that they follow the concept of similar free schools in Sweden. By introducing such diversity into the school system, the government hoped it would encourage innovation and 'galvanize' improvement. They were automatically academies and, so, benefited from the same freedoms and were subject to the same assessments as state school academies that had converted. It is currently too early to know the impact of these.

Teaching schools

Teaching schools were introduced by the government in 2010. Their designation was to be part of the remit of the National College (NC, 2011b). The aim of these schools, led by outstanding leaders, was to play a significant part in locality wide school improvement. They were expected to spread expertise in teaching and to manage staff development and contribute to initial teacher training (see also Chapter 3). They were expected to provide support for vulnerable schools by either working as a support school themselves or, if not, then brokering support for schools in their locality on their behalf. By doing so, they would eventually be expected to undertake the brokering role previously undertaken by the LAs. Selection criteria were rigorously adhered to and included schools which had gained outstanding in their latest OFSTED inspection for leadership, teaching and learning, and overall effectiveness. The first 100 schools were to be designated by September 2011.

Factors impacting on the success of system leadership

Successive government policy suggests a favourable climate for encouraging heads to undertake roles as system leaders, but it has been identified that they also must have the required knowledge and understanding (NCSL, 2007) of how to do so. In addition, they need to be encouraged to do so for the policy to succeed. A question to ask, however, is to what extent is undertaking system leadership a conscious attempt by headteachers to facilitate reforms on behalf of government because they believe in them for their intrinsic worth, or are there other more extrinsic forms of motivation? Why would headteachers seek to extend their role in ways that could be seen to lead to further work intensification? These are questions addressed in Part 2 and Part 3 of this book.

Another factor for successful system leadership is related to the capacity within the school that needs to be built and secured so that the system leadership of the headteacher does not adversely impact on the school in which they are substantive head (NCSL, 2007). The use of NLEs as system leaders stems from recognition by government of the need for sustainability of the reform and the move away from 'superheads' to the use of support schools. In using the experience of the staff of the support school, it places less pressure on the consultant headteacher to be the sole means of school improvement in the supported school and, thus, alleviates some of the criticism of the use of a single 'superhead'.

A cautionary note regarding the capacity within federations is the speed at which they grow. Many are performance federations and, so, work by taking over failing schools. Hill (2010) argues that chains should ensure capacity with enough successful schools in their group before undertaking to support others. Moving too quickly without building sufficient capacity across the schools before taking on another school could be detrimental to the federation. Ways in which schools can be seen to build capacity are to become a 'learning organization' (Mulford, 2003), to distribute leadership (Harris, 2009) and to ensure an effective process for succession management which can be extended to include managing succession and staff development across schools (Hargreaves, 2010).

3 Changing Roles: Leadership, Management and CPD

The headteacher's leadership qualities and skills are a critical factor in the effective performance of a school (Bush, 2008a). New contexts in single institutions or system leadership across schools has led to changing permanent and temporary leadership roles, which have brought changing perspectives on the nature of school leadership. However, while educational reforms have changed their working practices, the headteachers' role has continued to be pivotal. They are used as one of the main levers for school transformation, as they act as agents of change implementing government policy in schools. How school leaders exercise leadership and the models and styles they adopt is, therefore, significant to our understanding of the extent to which reforms are successfully implemented.

From the beginning of New Labour in 1997, there has been a massive increase in the amount of continuing professional development (CPD) offered to the profession, particularly in the form of programmes designed to prepare leaders for specific roles in middle and senior leadership. The National College opening in 2000 has been influential in the commissioning, development and delivery of leadership development for school leaders at different levels. The white paper (DfE,

2010b) introduced the concept of Teaching Schools, which would fundamentally change the leadership training and development of teachers. This chapter focuses on both the type of leadership being advocated to lead schools successfully and some of the various forms of leadership development in England.

Leadership and management

School leaders practice leadership and management, and both are needed for the effective performance of a school. Cuban (1988) is widely acknowledged as providing an early definition of the distinction between leadership and management. In essence, he argued that management operations translate the aims and intentions of policy and defined them in terms of the efficient maintenance of a system. Although good management will involve the skills of leadership, it is the element of change which makes leadership distinct. In contrast to management, leadership involves the formulation of change policies and the influence of others. For some, leadership and management are a 'fabricated binary' (Gunter, 2008, 262), and Bush (2003, 2008b) emphasizes that the management functions of a school should not be carried out without the values that underpin them. Despite this important element of management theory, as the leadership of heads is viewed as a critically important lever for implementing government policies, it is to the area of leadership that this chapter now turns.

Leadership models

Related to the varied nature of school leadership, and particularly the increasing complexity of the role of headteacher, there is no single theory of leadership which can be applied and several 'perspectives may be valid simultaneously' (Bush, 2008b, 8). It is not the purpose of this chapter to define or categorize the many types of leadership, but to consider those which have been identified as being required for the effective practice of leadership and have allowed headteachers to manage their changing roles effectively.

Transactional and transformational leadership

A transactional leader is concerned with an organization's outcomes and mainly tasks focussed often delegating their completion to others (Harris, 2005). Bush (2008b) argues that while there may be an exchange of reward for effort which benefits both parties, the process is limited by not engaging staff further than the specifics of the transaction. The disadvantage of this form of leadership in a period of rapid change is that it isn't able to adapt quickly enough (Day et al., 2000). As schools were restructured into more complex organizations with greater self management and levels of autonomy, there was a perceived need for a form of leadership which suited the level of transformation taking place (Gronn, 2003), involving changes to the relationships and interaction between headteachers and those they lead.

The model of transformational leadership is essentially collegiate in its approach and seeks to understand the ways in which influence rather than direction is used in leadership practice (Bush, 2008b). Transformational leaders build the relationships that motivate and inspire followers. Gaining the support of colleagues is important, as the role of the headteacher becomes more strategic and their influence has to continue, often in their absence. This doesn't preclude the view that such leaders existed in the past, but merely emphasizes their importance now and in the future. However, not all observers believe it is always for mutual benefit, as transformational leaders can become obsessed with their own vision (Bryman, 1992) or that required merely to implement government policy (Bush, 2008a), and this can lead to less of a shared and more of an imposed vision regarding school aims, organization and values.

Burns (1978) separated transactional and transformational leadership. This view of them as distinct is not shared by more recent observers, as the pace of change and rise of managerialism has increased the complexity of the leadership of the headteacher. Leadership is contextualised and contingent (Leithwood et al., 2006) and within the same school context, headteachers are likely to include both types of leadership in their practice.

One example is that they will be transactional leaders when ensuring the routine systems of the school are functioning but will combine this with transformational leadership in the way they inspire and motivate staff. A different example is that transformational leadership may be required to influence others where a school has been identified as failing, and needs to change quickly, but the practice used may be uni-directional in terms of managing people or 'top down' and, therefore, transactional.

Post-transformational leadership and collegiality

The complexity of modern headship from the turn of the twenty-first century led to the claim that the existing theoretical framework of leadership didn't reflect the role of school leaders and that a new model was required. Day et al. (2000) suggested a model called 'post-transformational leadership'. This model is distinct from transformational leadership in that it involves headteachers winning the commitment of staff and cooperation rather than merely their compliance. Influence is an integral part of post-transformational leadership. Influence can be 'intentional' (Yukl, 2002) and it is used as such in this sense, as it is exerted over others and generated in the form of relationships or expertise.

Simkins (2005) suggests that in the future collaboration and the use of co-operation will be more necessary than the use of formal hierarchical power. There is a 'reciprocal' interdependency involved in 'collaborated leadership' (Spillane et al., 2005, 39). Each party working in collaboration between or across schools must cooperate and agree on roles and leadership practice for the input to be most effective. Collegiate and collaborative leadership, there-fore, are a form of leadership particularly suited for those engaged in system leadership in federations and formal and informal collaborative clusters of schools.

Circumstances may dictate the degree of collegiality headteachers can undertake, in that some situations of failure may mean that staff need to be more directed. Collegiality is complicated when there are other imperatives that drive headteachers, such as their accountability for the national agenda. In these circumstances, heads may be less benign in winning staff commit-ment and become manipulative in their approach to ensure compliance. There is a hybrid, which is the operation of a collegial approach by headteach-ers until it becomes necessary to take action to satisfy the requirements of externally mandated policy (Wallace, 2001).

The moral dimension: management of change, compliance, strategy and guilt

The role of moral leadership is becoming increasing 'significant' in leadership in the twenty-first century and partly because of a belief that school lead-ers should adopt an 'ethical approach to decision making' (Bush, 2010). The strap line of the National College in 2011 was 'inspiring leaders to improve children's lives' and so emphasized the moral leadership and moral purpose which it expected should underpin the leadership practice of headteachers. Leading morally in an educational context involves the courage to act according to personally held principles and ethics and is values driven. Leadership practice includes taking ethical decisions about the distribution of resources or management of people (Begley, 2009) as heads lead organizations. Finding a balance between accommodating the agenda and leading with moral purpose can lead to compliance and guilt.

Compliance and change

Headteachers have had to manage unremitting change since the ERA and increasing complexity in the way the role of headteachers has changed. Change in the last 20 years has been both 'simultaneous' and 'multiple' (Southworth, 2008) and brought with it tensions between welcomed or opposed change and anticipated and unplanned change (Garrett, 1997). The management of change in schools is an important aspect of successful managerial leadership and is essential to implementing government legislation. Whether the changes to the headteachers' role have been chosen by them, such as the decision to undertake an external role, or imposed on them, such as the introduction of a children's centre on site, the way in which headteachers interpret change through their judgement of it, and commitment to it, must affect the way they implement its requirements. To what extent are headteachers committed to implementing change through intrinsic belief in the policy or because they have to comply?

Some tensions can occur with the need to reconcile change incurred, due to external imposition such as accommodating the test agenda or which may conflict with the values of the school. To manage this tension, headteachers may adopt a 'principled pragmatism' (Moore et al., 2002) as they try to find a balance between managing the education reform agenda and their own educational philosophy. In this way, they are open to new ideas but also aware of, and take account of, the way in which these will impact on the needs of their pupils.

The extent to which reforms will be successful must depend on the understanding heads have of what is expected and their ability to implement them. This *per se* implies that the reform measures are themselves formulated to ensure school improvement. It may be the case that it is the measures such as standardized testing rather than heads' failure to understand them or implement them effectively which is the root of any failure to use them successfully.

In this case, the blame for failure should be attached to the system and not the individual.

Mediating change and manipulating policy

Where policy has been imposed on headteachers there have been some opportunities for manoeuvre either provided consciously or unconsciously by the policy-makers or taken by the headteachers who have interpreted the policy to suit the requirements of their context. Opportunities for interpreting government policy can be due to its maintaining a degree of remoteness from the lives of those who enact it within schools (Leggett, 1997). The mediation of externally mandated policy by heads may be a conscious choice to act in a given situation because they have weighed up the factors and feel a course of action is the best one to take or just evolve over time. An example of this is workforce reform. Appraisal was a requirement for many years, but formed a small part if any in inspection, and so headteachers' responses to it ranged from largely following it, adapting it, and adopting a wider more inclusive approach to staff development and training or ignoring it altogether.

Bottery (2007, 162, original emphasis) agues that 'there will always be *some* room for interpretation, selection and mediation of policy directives' even with the most 'deterministic' of government policy, total control over implementation is not practical. Therefore, moral leadership can be utilized as heads manage the expectations and prescriptions to which they are subject while still finding space to take action in which they believe.

There is also a consideration which needs to be made by headteachers in managing imposed change regarding the consequences of not doing so. The SEF is an example of policy which was imposed but wasn't mandatory. Only the self-evaluation of the school was mandatory. However, not to do so was a risk for heads because of the expectation by OFSTED that it will be in place. The consequence of failing to produce a SEF was the potentially negative view inspectors would take of school's leadership and the impact this would have on the school's grading in inspection. This, in turn, would impact on the extent to which heads would be able to exercise their autonomy.

Stress and guilt

If heads are forced to undertake change which they do not agree with, they can suffer from feelings of guilt and self betrayal (Bottery, 2004). They may feel a sense of failure in that they haven't managed to accommodate the agenda in the best interests of their schools. In this form, guilt becomes unproductive, both at a personal and system level, as it can lead to disaffected heads leaving the system, causing a crisis in recruitment. If leadership is contingent on context, then leaders must understand both the context and the nature of leadership required to respond to it. School leadership development and preparation programmes have been devised to equip school leaders to understand the educational agenda and mediate pressures from it. Whether mediating pressure is to ensure the implementation of the policy against opposition or mediating pressure to conform is up to individuals and circumstances.

Leadership practice: distributed leadership

Distributed leadership in schools is the expansion of leadership to those who do not hold formal leadership roles (Harris, 2009). Bryman (1992) suggests that the transformational leader often demonstrates a 'charismatic' style of leadership which, if it leads to a 'hero' head approach rather than a collegiate one, has been discredited (Southworth, 2008). If the influence of leaders is only uni-directional from the headteacher to staff, as it is being suggested in the singular hero head model, then the leadership of the head would be difficult to sustain with the extensive managerial agenda of headship. The centrality of leadership is an important component of an effective school. This, of course, is not the same as that centrality being located in the position of the headteacher, but instead is located in a group of school leaders.

Harris (2008) cautions against the use of distributed leadership as a term to describe any form of shared leadership in schools or that everyone in schools will lead. Nevertheless, distributing leadership through empowering and motivating others to lead, and that leadership is not only located in the role of an individual such as the headteacher, has been identified as a mechanism for creating effective organizational change (Spillane, 2006). Distributed leadership assumes that the head will share leadership in practice with others and that their participation will lead to school improvement. Distributed leadership is not restricted to those in senior positions but can be transferred from one tier of leadership to others. So the Senior Leadership Team (SLT) can distribute leadership to middle leaders, and so on. Hargreaves (2010, 15) argues distributed leadership has 'an emphasis on preparing leaders at every level'.

Headteachers are being encouraged to distribute leadership as the system transforms. System redesign has led to new forms of system leadership across schools and an increasing complexity in the role of school leader. Such leadership is unlikely to be successfully implemented through the 'top-down' approach synonymous with the sole leadership of the headteacher. To facilitate new forms of leadership practice, headteachers are required to have good interpersonal skills, as their influence has to be practised through their relationships and interactions with staff. This is true for all heads but is especially true for system leaders, who frequently have to be an absent presence as they lead across schools and ensure others are leading when they are away. To facilitate this, heads need 'emotional intelligence' (Goleman, 1995). However, while having emotional intelligence may give headteachers a degree of understanding of situations, it doesn't guarantee that they necessarily exercise it in their leadership.

System leadership is further complicated by the practice of leaders in school other than the head, who have formal or informal leadership roles in other schools. This can lead to leadership being distributed both within and across schools in collaborations and federations. The importance of distributed leadership lies not in what is distributed but '*how*' it is distributed (Harris, 2009, original emphasis). The extent to which distributed leadership is allowed to happen in schools is ultimately located in the power of the headteacher (Hatcher, 2005). However, in a distributed leadership framework, both headteachers and others in formal leadership roles would act as 'gatekeepers' to the practice of distributed leadership (Harris, 2008). Headteachers need to consider who will be involved and when and plan and evaluate distributed practice carefully for organizational effectiveness.

Leadership development

Leadership preparation is considered important to ensure high-quality leadership and the effectiveness of schools (Bush, 2008b). The professional development of school leaders is not a new phenomenon. It has been used during the timeline for research for this book as a tool for government to train and advise school leaders to understand fully the management demands of their job. As the managerial and entrepreneurial role of heads began to grow as a result of Local Management of Schools (LMS), so, too, did the opportunities for training. Headlamp was introduced in 1995, which provided headteachers in their first year of headship with funding to spend on training determined by self-identification of professional development needs. This began a process of ensuring a more equal entitlement to professional development and it was followed by the National Professional Qualification for Headship (NPQH), and the Standards for Headteachers (Teacher Training Agency, 1997; 1998; DfES, 2004c). As well as standards-based programmes, the Training Development Agency (TDA) developed a Leadership Programme for Serving Headteachers (LPSH) in 1998, but while this was available, it wasn't compulsory.

Professional development at this time was piecemeal and depended largely on the will of individual schools and the extent to which headteachers wished to access it either for themselves or others. While preparation for leadership was in place, it was the election of New Labour in 1997 that heralded a real increase in funding for, and availability of, leadership preparation training and programmes. This reflected the increased importance and recognition of leadership and school leaders in particular as levers to implement school reforms. Many training providers for leadership development and training have arisen since. Leadership development was undertaken within collaborative partnerships, such as trusts or federations. An example is the Harris Federation, which offers its own MA qualification aligned to its way of working. Whether or not this limits understanding to the instructional leadership contained within the group is debatable. It could potentially close off opportunities to learn from alternative practice. However, it is the role of the National College that has been the most significant in the professional development of school leaders.

The National College

The year 2000 saw the opening of the then-Prime Minister Tony Blair's brainchild, The National College for School Leadership (NCSL). The establishment of the National College in 2000 and its continuation after the election of the Coalition government in 2010 can be recognized as evidence of government's commitment to school leadership. The National College was given responsibility for all the national leadership programmes for the training of school leaders at different stages of their development. This ranges from emergent or those not yet assistant and deputy heads through to consultant leadership for those school leaders who are involved in school-to-school support.

The role of consultant leader the final stage of leadership recognized by National College was recognized by the DfES in both the role of Primary Strategy Consultant Leader (PSCL) and consultant leadership through the London Challenge (DfES, 2003e). PSCLs were introduced through the Primary Leadership Programme (DfES, 2003d) which was launched as part of the Primary National Strategy, with training provided by the NCSL through LAs for heads to act as consultants in schools deemed as vulnerable. A national consultant leader course of 5 days was also available, delivered by the NCSL. While there isn't a specific leadership training course for NLEs there is for LLEs, and they undertake a training programme at the National College subsequent to their identification by their LA.

One of the National College's challenges from the government has been to manage leadership succession. This problem has been partly created as a result of the imminent retirement of the 'baby boomer' generation born in the early 1950s. Approximately 45 per cent of headteachers are eligible to retire by 2013. Another critical factor is the lack of ambition to become headteachers by those who are in senior leadership roles and who it could be assumed are their natural successors. This may explain the raft of leadership programmes and training opportunities offered to aspiring leaders such as those by the National College (National Professional Qualification for Headship; Leadership Pathways; Trainee and Associate Heads Programme), many of which require the involvement and experience of practising headteachers for their delivery. School leaders were being encouraged through National College training programmes to develop a coaching and mentoring approach suited to the collegiate or moral model of leadership.

In addition, leadership has been distributed to senior and middle management teams due to the increasing complexity of the leadership of headteachers with system leadership and multi-agency working causing their work to be intensified. The role of those in leadership positions other than headteacher has been recognized by the NC as an important contributory factor to school improvement and effectiveness. This is evident from the National College's leadership programme devoted to middle leaders 'Leading from the Middle', and its moves in 2010 to encourage schools to lead or be part of a cluster aimed at developing middle leadership in partnership with the National College.

In 2009, its remit was broadened to respond to the wider Children's Services agenda and renamed The National College for Leadership of Schools and Children's Services and generally referred to as National College. A leadership programme for those involved in leading children's services was subsequently developed. The National Professional Qualification in Integrated Centre Leadership (NPQICL) was previously developed to cater for those leading in multi-agency or early year's organizations. As school leadership became more complex, the college tried to reflect the professional development needs of system leaders. One example was the pilot Primary Executive Headship Programme (NC, 2010), aimed at providing leadership development for aspiring or current executive headteachers. The college became an executive agency as a result of a change of remit by the Coalition (NC, 2011b).

Teaching schools

Teaching schools, introduced in the white paper (DfE, 2010b), will lead 'the training and professional development of teachers and head teachers' (20). The role of the college was to identify and designate schools with the appropriate leadership to become teaching schools. These schools are part of the continuing theme of the Coalition to decentralize the school system and encourage a self-improving system (see Chapter 2). The role of teaching schools is expected to have a significant impact on succession management. They will be able to recruit trainee teachers and identify talent in the local cluster helping to train staff by offering CPD opportunities and retain talent for the local area.

Part 2
Changing School Organizations and Roles for Headteachers

The Development of New Roles for Headteachers

It is well documented that schools have had to deal with constant and unremitting change in the period following the ERA (1988), which showed no sign of diminishing with the latest change of government in 2010. As schools respond to wider system changes, there have been changes to the role of headteachers. This chapter focuses on the forces behind the changing role of heads, analyzes the factors they considered in undertaking new roles and their changing relationships with governors and parents.

All change: the role of the government

Change was an expectation for all heads, as typified by this example:

> The expectations for a school, never mind a head, are there will be another lot of legislation soon just as you are getting your head around the last lot. There will

> be another 'Excellence and Enjoyment' or another 'Every Child Matters' or maybe
> another National Curriculum revamp, and it is all a bit of a shifting carpet, and you
> have to try to keep your balance as head. (Ht 16)

The reasons why headteachers have reacted in a particular way to change are less well known. Bush (2008a) attests that leadership is increasingly linked with the personal and professional values of the leaders themselves, but that, predominantly, headteachers have what is to be valued 'imposed' on them by the policies of the government. Morris (2001) promised the introduction of a period of 'earned autonomy' for heads of effective schools, a theme continued by the Coalition government in 2010. They promised to free heads from bureaucracy, particularly that from the LAs, in the belief that this would allow them time to devote to raising standards of teaching and learning. Was the autonomy promised by either government dependent on heads successfully implementing a known political agenda?

Heads recognised the dilemma between the extent to which they have been able to lead according to their own values and beliefs in the best interests of the schools they lead, and the barriers imposed by policy to achieving this:

> It's difficult to know what's driving me now. Whether I am doing things the way I
> would do them anyway, or whether I am being driven by external forces. It's dif-
> ficult to say if it is the government or me. (Ht 18)

The role of national government in the change process was discussed by all the headteachers. There was general acknowledgement that whatever change was initiated, 'it will be to the agenda which suits the government' (Ht 17), and:

> I can't imagine it would be an easy thing for schools to develop or change just as
> they want to do unless it fits in with the government's ideas. (Ht 3)

There was a general belief that government, while clearly needing to please the electorate (Levin, 2003), might also consider what is in the best interests of improving education. Unfortunately, it was also widely believed that their intentions didn't match reality:

> I am sure they [government] want the best . . . but I wonder how many lessons
> are learned from things that they put in that go wrong and especially those which
> are preventable? (Ht 14)

She later added that as government was unable to anticipate the consequences of its policy, it should 'depoliticize education' (Ht 14).

An example of unintended consequences was workload following the introduction of workforce reform, a process described as:

> a monumental mess which they just didn't anticipate, that doesn't work in practice. (Ht 16)

There was also the view that while government would determine the change it wanted to see and design the policy to implement it, the detail and process is sometimes left to the profession. An example of this was the introduction of ECM and extended schools. Detail is left to the profession to sort out, because as a 'complex adaptive challenge' (Heifetz, 1994) there is at the time no known solution or one which can be easily adapted. The system has been allowed to evolve with heads used as agents of change:

> I think what will happen is that heads doing extended provision will lead it. They will find a solution and that will then become a pattern of practice . . . More and more, that's how solutions are found and I think it's quite shocking how little real thought is given to how education policy will work. I think it's a bit of a wing and a prayer every time. (Ht 15)

> The government is working on the process of not solving anything. We solve the problem for them and then they say OK, yes, that's fine and we'll go with that . . . in the last 5–6 years practice has outstripped policy by miles and is accelerating away. (Ht 23)

The removal of bureaucracy by both governments and the opportunities for autonomy particularly from the LA were very well received. There was some optimism that the Coalition was seeking to reduce some of the burdens of leadership:

> Some people believe that nothing ever good comes out of the government, but actually it does. If you can really reduce bureaucracy for your staff, this is a good idea of government's and we should applaud it. But it's like anything it is about how it is implemented. (Ht 11)

Speculating on the future of leadership

All the heads speculated about how future models of school leadership would develop when describing their own role change. There was some difference over the course of the interview cycle regarding the extent to which the interviewees could visualize the future roles of heads, as well as a range in terms of the amount of change. At the beginning of the interview cycle, one head speculated:

> There could be different models, but I think that would be really difficult to monitor in practice. (Ht 3)

Even in the second round of interviews, some heads, while feeling that change was inevitable, still weren't quite sure what it would be:

> I don't think the traditional model of one head – one school will be in operation forever because it won't work like that I don't think. (Ht 17)

Defining terms was often confusing at the beginning of a cycle of change, as illustrated from rounds two and three:

> Well I don't really know now what an executive head is. (Ht 8)
>
> I am not sure of the language [collaboration or federation] at the moment as it is all a bit like shifting sands. (Ht 11)

Heads were well aware of the government's agenda by the beginning of 2011. It was recognized that the agenda was ideological as well as educational and that change would be major and swift rather than slow and incremental:

> I think a new government has to make its mark and to leave behind a legacy that is easily identifiable to that political machine. I think it is unfortunate that they used the same name [academy] for something that had been used by the previous administration because it complicates it for families or for those who don't understand or have time for the politics. (Ht 20)

Autonomy with a reduction in bureaucracy quickly became a theme of the Coalition government. It was greeted with a variety of scepticism and hope:

> I think as heads we need to watch this space because I don't think we know enough about it. It depends whether it's a genuine kind of freedom. (Ht 14)

Heads noted that following the support from the white paper (DfE, 2010b) and changes to school structures there would be more school to school support in a variety of contexts. They were positive about the process and their participation in the change:

> What I think will happen is . . . outstanding schools will be asked to help satisfactory schools through the [academy] process. (Ht 22)
>
> I am pleased they have recognized the strength and the positive nature of successful schools supporting others in successful situations. (Ht 14)

It was suggested that a two-tier system might be developing and that some less proactive heads could get left behind:

> I think there is a real dilemma with some colleagues who don't understand the system as it is with the roles of executive head and federations and school support . . . Some of them seem to think in the here and now . . . They aren't thinking about what they are going to do in the future to move on. (Ht 24)

The pivotal role of the headteacher in the future

The role of a single heroic headteacher who leads on most if not all issues in school has been increasingly perceived as unsustainable (Harris, 2008) or untenable (Southworth, 2008). The pivotal role of the headteacher in the future of school leadership was speculated on at length with reference to a variety of contexts. This led to the identification of several issues:

> Whether a single headteacher in every school is necessary.
>
> Whether or not a school leader needs to have qualified teacher status (QTS).
>
> If school leaders are to lead more than one institution, should they also have QTS and, if not, who should?

The majority view of heads was that there had to be someone leading one or more schools who had QTS. Only a small minority of headteachers were prepared to accept or to be open to the idea that someone who was not a qualified teacher could lead a school:

> I don't believe you have to have been a teacher to be a headteacher. I have always thought that. (Ht 20)

> Parents need to be assured their children's education is going to be the best, but who organises it doesn't have to be a teacher any more than a football manager has to be the best footballer. (Ht 21)

One head also stressed the proviso that such a leader had to have the 'right personality to lead and motivate with vision' (Ht 9). In addition was the belief that if the school leader wasn't a teacher they had to employ someone to lead learning that had an educational background:

> Whatever happens in the future you will still have a lead educational professional whatever they are called . . . deputy, head or lead learner. (Ht 15)

The majority of heads were against the idea of school leaders being other than qualified teachers:

> I don't think standards would be good enough without professional teacher training. (Ht 18)
>
> I believe 100 per cent it has got to be a headteacher that was a great class teacher, because for me the role is nothing else but teaching and learning . . . If you move away from that as an executive headteacher it would be very difficult to improve quality. (Ht 27)
>
> I think you can delegate many of the other roles but you have to know about your staff and how they deliver, what the content is, and how you can make it better. I can't see that if you had someone who came without a teaching background they could manage that. (Ht 17)

The development of new roles: headteachers' perceptions

Four issues were identified:

> Spreading best practice to support other schools
> Succession management and headship
> The viability of small schools
> Every Child Matters

The reasons for identification are described in turn as follows:

Spreading best practice to support other schools

Working to support vulnerable and failing schools was recognized as one reason for heads' changing roles. They noted a range of factors for their involvement:

> I suppose someone must have thought that a lot of schools are doing great things and why aren't we sharing this? (Ht 18)

> I think we as heads have a responsibility to our children as a whole community so we should be working together on that aspect of it. (Ht 7)

Heads believed that school-to-school support was potentially an effective lever in the system for raising standards by improving vulnerable schools:

> But what we have seen is that head-to-head and school-to-school work balances the challenge and support so brilliantly. Headteachers become more confident, are willing to have help that isn't hit and run national strategy type help. It continues and gets embedded in the school. It is system wide and system led. (Ht 27)

Generally heads believed that support worked best if it was welcomed:

> I like school-to-school support so long as the school receiving the support can invite it in the right way so that it's not forced on them but is collaboration between the schools. (Ht 25)

However, while supportive of colleagues in difficulty, the heads were also unequivocal that their support had parameters, which were not to support either indefinitely or for a lost cause.

The continuing demise of the LAs was highlighted as an important reason for the likely increase in system support from schools. This was either from individuals schools supporting others as collaborations, or for federations and chains of schools to work as academies or otherwise (see Chapter 5).

Succession management and headship

Headteachers commented on the development of new opportunities for them being a result of the imminent retirement of the 'baby boomer' generation and the need to plan for their succession:

> I think they are panicking and witless about what is going to happen in the future with headteachers. (Ht 19)

> Because they haven't got enough heads coming through have they? That's the bottom line. (Ht 16)

Heads believed that the crisis was more than just people retiring, in that the job of headship itself was unattractive and either causing people to leave or failing to attract successors:

> They see models of heads who are worn out and tired and they don't want the job for themselves. (Ht 27)
>
> I think they have to be more proactive in looking at ways of ensuring succession. My three assistant heads don't want to be heads. (Ht 7)
>
> You are only one major parental complaint away from suspension. You are only one poor inspection or difficult governing body away from losing your headship . . . and there aren't enough people coming through education wanting to do the job anymore. (Ht 25)

For some headteachers, the blame for a lack of interest in headship was placed firmly on the mishandling of the system by successive governments, which had lost the trust of the profession:

> There is a lot of talent around, and there is a lot of talent coming through, so what is the reason they aren't interested? Have we put people off leadership by some of the things we have demanded of headteachers or some of the policy decisions that have been made? (Ht 12)
>
> I think for many it is the lack of respect. The fact that heads are made a scapegoat for every issue is a factor which puts people off doing it. (Ht 17)

Ht 23 agreed with and quoted Ball (1990) in his views of a 'discourse of derision' being perpetrated against the profession by government through the media.

Some heads with experience of international placements believed that school leaders in other countries were more valued:

> It was fascinating in other countries because people really valued heads . . . Heads and teachers had much more status in terms of respect, but that has been a media issue around education over here for many, many years actually. (Ht 12)

There was a contrasting view from one head, who, echoing a view of headship supported by Etzioni (1969), thought that the profession had become more 'semi professional', thus making it less attractive to successors:

> We have become like glorified operators in a factory. We are not seen to be professional; therefore, we are not trusted, and therefore, we need parents to come in and tell us how to run the place and that's not the answer. (Ht 5)

Irrespective of the pressure they felt as individuals, all headteachers put some of the blame for lack of interest in headship on the system of accountability and the pressure to perform (see Chapter 6). There was a distinction between a general lack of enthusiasm for the role and a disinclination for headship in challenging situations where:

> They can't get heads for schools like ours . . . with all the shootings and the stabbings. (Ht 8)

Co-headship was identified as a means of managing the crisis of succession:

> Shared headship is another way . . . It's a good idea. If you are moving towards retirement, why should the school lose all that expertise? (Ht 18)

Encouraging heads to lead more than one school was discussed by almost all heads as a solution to the future lack of leadership:

> I think the future of headship is going to be that you are not just head of one school. I think, from a sustainability point of view, there won't be enough people who want to become headteachers because the role doesn't appeal to many staff. (Ht 17)
>
> I think federations will grow because no one wants the job anymore and it is becoming too chaotic. (Ht 25)

A small minority of heads believed that finding leaders to lead across schools would be potentially difficult:

> . . . and they will struggle to fill these roles of one head for several schools; it's a very different way of working. (Ht 7)

One head in a rural context thought it worked well only because of his particular circumstances:

> I am not so sure about federations generally, because this one is working for specific reasons such as using someone known and experienced like me in this community. (Ht 21)

Headteachers 4 and 7 believed that federations were neither inevitable nor beneficial as a means of solving the problem of succession. Their view was based on the lack of visibility of the head in the community:

> I am not sure it works . . . I mean, I am on the playground every morning and in the corridors. People identify with me and I am not sure you can do that . . . in fact, I am sure you can't do that if you are head of federated schools. (Ht 4)

Otherwise, heads believed that colleagues would want to lead across several schools as they did themselves. Even if the system attracts enough leaders, several heads were concerned about 'what quality are we getting' (Ht 11) 'in a scarcity market' (Ht 21) when future leaders are chosen from a much smaller available pool of recruits? Heads believed it was their role and moral purpose to improve leadership succession:

> Schools and heads have to take that responsibility and most schools think it's someone else's responsibility to promote the job to a new generation of headteachers. (Ht 27)

The viability of small schools

Establishing long-term or permanent collaborations between schools has been identified as being an important structural development, due to viability and financial constraint (Hill and Matthews, 2008). It is more difficult to recruit to small schools, and particularly in the Catholic sector with its more stringent recruitment requirements (NCSL, 2006). As this head notes:

> I don't think long term small schools can survive in the same way, and I think soft federations are the answer. I think they will get to that point through failure and necessity. For example, they aren't going to find enough headteachers for the one-form entry Catholic schools. The incentive isn't there for deputies of large schools to go for headships of smaller schools. (Ht 5)

Heads of three-form entry schools commented that they didn't find their own role undoable and directly attributed their view to the benefits of economies of scale. These leaders benefited from a bigger budget and the opportunity to afford more or higher-paid senior staff to be more strategic in their own roles (see Chapter 7). There was some recognition by them that colleagues in small schools might be less fortunate and would have to 'think about either networking or sharing the load somehow' (Ht 10). Federation was identified as a way of doing this for a 'group of small rural schools' (Ht 13) and Ht 16, who had also experienced small school headship, argued:

> I don't think there is any doubt about it that with too few school leaders they will have to federate. (Ht 16)

Heads of small schools shared these views because:

> As a head, I still have to have responsibilities with [curriculum] areas, as we just don't have enough people. (Ht 9)
>
> I am not just federated head, I am also federated SENCO and core subject coordinator because I just haven't got the staff to do it' (Ht 25)

Nevertheless, she was also able to argue that the strategic benefits brought through federation had mitigated issues with workload (see Chapter 7).

Every Child Matters

Every Child Matters (DfES, 2003a), from which followed *The Children's Act* (DfES, 2004a) and *The Education Act* (DfES, 2006), provided opportunities for new roles for school leaders. In the first two rounds, ECM was identified as bringing with its introduction, new roles for them and new ways of working and relationships with others as well as potential changes to the curriculum.

Headteachers' motivations for undertaking new roles

Many heads combined a new model of leadership in school with an extensive external role. This matches the findings of Chapman et al. (2008), who found that school leaders were undertaking a 'combination' of roles. It is, therefore, difficult to determine any single motivation for either internal or external roles because, for some heads, the motivations are complicated and involve several different reasons, depending on the type of role and whether it was imposed or chosen by them.

Leadership of a children's centre was imposed, but all other roles were undertaken voluntarily. Heads took advantage of opportunities made available to them through government policy together with encouragement from National College, TDA, DCSF/DfE and LAs.

The responses of the heads as to why they undertake new roles form the basis of the subheadings:

> Moral purpose
>
> Professional challenge and development
>
> Financial considerations

Moral purpose

Leading with moral purpose was a key motivator identified by all heads involved in school-to-school support. They all believed that doing so enabled them to help children and colleagues:

> There is definitely a wider moral purpose of why we are doing this. That is the key for me that runs through setting up things for all three schools in a family of academies. This is going to give a good educational experience to 1,000 children. (Ht 11)
>
> I have to say, the main driver is moral purpose. You are doing what you are doing in an outstanding setting for all the children if you can. But the way the system is developing now, you can do it for more children. (Ht 26)

Moral purpose was linked to personal satisfaction in succeeding in other schools:

> I know when I went in there it would have definitely been special measures, so it has shifted and that is a great sense of achievement. (Ht 13)
>
> You start to see a change and that's what keeps you going. (Ht 5)

School-to-school support was felt to be more beneficial and more driven by moral purpose than that of those who support schools through the accountability system. The role of SIP was abolished in 2010 but had been experienced by the heads:

> NLE is about supporting rather than, you know, what a SIP's role seems to be, which just seems to be challenging only and just data driven. (Ht 14)

The judgemental role of OFSTED without consequential school improvement was abhorrent for heads:

> No, I didn't like the OFSTED role. I did a few inspections and I didn't like it at all. I found the whole punitive aspect of the role difficult. (Ht 17)
>
> No, I wouldn't do it, because I don't like the relationship between OFSTED inspectors and schools. (Ht 5)

There were a few exceptions to this view of OFSTED. Ht 18 'waves the flag' for them and Ht 12 had a pragmatic approach and inspects schools because she gains useful information to improve her own school.

Professional challenge and development

While not wanting to leave their schools permanently, heads identified their need for challenge:

> I love doing it because it gives me another perspective as to what is happening nationally apart from any reading . . . I would just be stifled otherwise. I wouldn't be able to stand it. (Ht 8)
>
> I wanted a challenge, I suppose. I think having both schools has put me out of my comfort zone and this is good for us because you can become complacent. (Ht 21)
>
> So, in terms of sustaining development and improvement, it has very much enabled me to still work in a challenging way without needing to leave a school to take on a different or new challenge. (Ht 20)

There was some evidence to substantiate the views of Gronn (2003) that leadership can become a treadmill. I would extend this judgement to suggest that system leadership can become addictive because of the drive of personal challenge:

> I feel in some ways in the last 4-5 years I have had so many opportunities I really want to try, it's like being let loose in a sweety shop. But there are so many, and I am so greedy to try all the new ones, that I have to learn to say no to some of them, but it is difficult. There is a limit not so much to what you can do, but to what you can do simultaneously. (Ht 19)

> I want to be an executive head of ten schools. I want to lead strategically and have heads in those schools. (Ht 22)

Financial considerations

Some heads chose to work in consultancy as a potential income stream, either after retirement or as a safety net 'if it goes wrong here' (Ht 7). For some executive heads of federations or collaborations, the external work was financially very rewarding and they were paid six-figure sums. For others who were seconded to schools or a federation head of two small schools, the rewards were not great in comparison for the work involved. Many heads highlighted the inequality:

> I got two points. I mean two points for two or three days a week. You wouldn't notice, and yet if they had to bring people in it would cost lots more. (Ht 13)
>
> I know a colleague who earns three times what I earn and of two who earn more than that . . . I think there are some people who earn a lot but there is a lot of disparity. (Ht 26)

It was recognized that supporting other schools was financially advantageous for the schools in supplementing the budget or economies of scale:

> I did consultancy, which was one day a week and two days a week for the LEA in 'Blake school' and others, at £300 per day. In doing that, I earned £17,000 to pay off my school's deficit. (Ht 16)
>
> In terms of economies of scale, it has had a huge impact on both schools. [Client school] had a deficit budget and it now has a carry forward and so now I don't think of one school but two, and the federation business manager can think of things on a much wider scale. (Ht 24)

These motivations are not hierarchical and it was apparent that many heads had a variety of reasons:

> I think challenge is the key to driving me, but moral purpose is why I am in teaching. (Ht 25)
>
> My main motivator is that I never think I am good enough. I don't think I have achieved what I needed to achieve which is part of my upbringing . . . I am

determined to be able to look back when I retire and say that I was part of something which changed education for the better. (Ht 23)

Characteristics of system leaders

Heads commented that there were certain characteristics which they believed were essential for effective system leadership. They all pointed to a need for 'political acumen' (Ht 23) and an ability to anticipate and translate the educational agenda into practice for their schools:

> One thing is what I would describe as the ability to become less parochial. I suspect to have a broader or more strategic view of the system outside your school, or the big picture, you need to have stepped out of your school to know what the job is. (Ht 14)

Heads had a relentless, highly focused attitude to the pursuit of excellence, either implied or frequently made explicit in their responses:

> We don't come out with excuses, and if something isn't right we say so and how to improve it and what we will do. We don't rest on our laurels. (Ht 24)
>
> I don't get involved with the minutia of anything. I am not a flibbertigibbet. I am not just constantly onto the next thing. (Ht 22)

An intolerance of failure was evident and heads applied high standards to their own work and to that of staff. They were also critical of systemic failure illustrated by this head, who spoke for many others:

> I upset a couple of governors and a few heads in a meeting recently when I said that we had failed children in the last ten years . . . we have been massively funded in the last few years, but we haven't made a comparable difference to children. We work harder, longer hours and do more but not smarter. (Ht 23)

An understanding of strategic leadership was considered an essential characteristic, as system leaders need to be an absent presence in their schools:

> X was my school for 5 years and I now have to watch [head of school] run things his way . . . To do that, you have to have emotional intelligence because you have to be accountable for everything but let other people do it. (Ht 23)

The sense of emotional attachment felt by some heads had to be managed:

> I think system leaders have to be happy with being unsettled and not psycho-
> pathic or care about that quite so much. You don't need to be owned by the staff
> quite so much and perhaps that comes with mature leadership. (Ht 26)

Leadership which is more detached often has to rely more on trust and good relationships with staff. Therefore, 'empathy' (Ht 14) for both the staff in their base school and supported schools was important:

> Even if you have to tell people they are failing, there is a way of doing it so they
> don't go off sick for three weeks. I think it's about knowing how to manage peo-
> ple and how you present things to people. (Ht 11)

Ht 13 argued about the importance of 'resilience'. Similarly:

> They [system leaders] are people who are driven and don't give up and thrive on
> the high of success. To get it you have to go through some pain on the way and
> you have to be able to sustain through the pain. Some people just don't want to
> be beaten up. (Ht 19)

Ht 22 suggested that, 'I think you don't get stressed', and Ht 20 that, 'I don't get diverted'.

One head suggested that the difference between system leadership and other effective headship was a question of 'depth' (Ht 25):

> You can be the head of a single school but not need the same sheer drive,
> determination, resilience, energy, enthusiasm and vision. You have got to be
> visionary. It's perception, as well. To be able to see instantly where the cracks
> are and act on it quickly and then to have the charisma and it is charisma to
> be able to take staff with you in both settings. Without a 'go out there and
> win them over' type of personality, staff wouldn't come and the school would
> crash. (Ht 25)

Changing partnerships: governors

Heads identified the needs of governors and parents. It is a feature of these relationships that they changed over the years, often due to their strategic importance and impact on the role of the headteachers.

It is important to draw a distinction between the attitude of headteachers towards the model of governance and their attitude to their individual governing bodies. The former drew universal lack of approval, but with some exceptions the relationships heads had with governors were good. While appreciating individuals, there was a perceived level of bureaucracy associated with keeping governors up to date, which was time consuming and frustrating for heads. One head commented that leading a large school in the 'big company bracket' meant some governors were 'out of their depth trying to cover the issues' (Ht 5). Another suggested this led to a greater workload for heads because of:

> the amount of time that I have to spend engaging with governors and other stake-holders. You are doing it, then you are writing it up and then you are evaluating it . . . some of the things we have to report to governors is a waste of time. (Ht 11)

Many heads appreciated their governor's support and that many governors were both knowledgeable and skilful:

> The governing body is a real strength of our school. They are very supportive of us, possibly because it is a church school and the culture of our school is strong. (Ht 9)
>
> We have very strong and capable governors here. (Ht 26)

The relationship heads experienced with the chair of governors was particularly important to them. This was either because the chair was poor and, so, hindered the work of the head unnecessarily or because the head was someone who could be trusted to be a critical friend. In one example, a chair of governors explained the advantages of federation to an OFSTED inspector who had hitherto been sceptical:

> He had a conversation on his own with Alfred who put him straight. It's interesting because as a chair of governors he could have a robust conversation in a way I couldn't as the head of schools. The inspector came out a changed man and thought federations were fantastic! (Ht 23)

The changing role of the governing body

The role of the governing body developed and extended from 2005, due both to the structural reform of schools and changes in the type of decisions it needed to consider regarding new roles for headteachers.

Decisions were taken with regard to new internal roles for heads in single institutions such as children's centres and co-locations, or system leadership, often accompanied by changes in the structure of the overall school organization. One headteacher who was contemplating the future of her co-location with a special school made this observation:

> It is down to governors because if they don't [federate], either because they don't think it's a good idea or they don't appoint the right person, then the whole concept of working as a new model will wither and die. (Ht 3)

Governors needed to be convinced that the school would be secure with the development of heads' roles and some heads faced opposition. The first example relates to working with a national agency and the other to academy conversion:

> Governors here are now very supportive. I think initially they were worried that I wasn't going to be here as much but now they are much better because we are still successful. (Ht 10)

> Oh yes, we had governors who gave me hell and one suggested it was seeking another logo on my belt . . . But they got really nasty and almost personal but the other governors could see through that. (Ht 22)

Alternatively, the governing body of one school was proactive in ways disapproved of by the headteacher:

> Unbeknown to me, my chair of governors expressed an interest [to DfE] in academy status . . .What scares me is that my GB [governing body] might railroad me into it. (Ht 25)

It might be the trust that the heads have built up with a proven track record of success as effective heads through inspection that has granted them overall support by the governors. However, it might also be a degree of fear on the part of governors due to a perceived crisis in recruiting future leaders. One chair of governors in the school led by Ht 13 was very positive about her wish to work in support of another school and felt that she should undertake more work to help local schools, but this degree of moral purpose was unusual and more likely was the need perceived by governors to retain their headteacher. The first two illustrations relate to setting up a federation and collaboration and the third to academy conversion:

> It all started when my chair of governors started to talk about what was going to happen if I leave. (Ht 23)
>
> What I think the governing bodies would say straight away and particularly the governing body from my first school is that it has been the most likely factor in me remaining in the school for longer. (Ht 20)
>
> The governing body allowed me to do this because they said, 'We trust you but we will only agree to go forward if we can have some guarantees that you will see us through with this'. (Ht 22)

In agreeing to changing school structures, governors were also agreeing to new models of governance.

New models of governance

Criticism of the system of governance to respond to the needs of system leadership was highlighted by heads in all rounds. As the number and variety of multiple collaborations increased, the role of the governors, pivotal to the process of their development, became critical:

> The governors' model is hopeless . . . and that is one of the things which appeals to me about academy status, the smaller governing body. (Ht 11)
>
> How do you run anything with 16 lay people who then also choose the next leader of the school? That's a bizarre system . . . Part of the federation was about an attack on governance not the governors themselves. (Ht 23)

The structure of governing bodies changed and their numbers were reduced for both federation and academy status. Change was largely driven by the chairs of governing bodies. If heads were in place, then this was also strongly driven by them. The key point is that the governing bodies of federations and long-term collaborations had been set up specifically for the purpose and were seen to be more effective. There were many different models of governance in federations and collaborations some of which are illustrated:

> We are five schools now with 14 governors but everything is delegated to a strategic governing committee of five. (Ht 23)
>
> The governing body which is a governing body of 12 has been stunning and much more strategic now than they ever were before we reconfigured for federation. They ask simple but really important questions and we hadn't had that before. (Ht 24)

Some governing bodies of federations were also actively pursuing the role and implications of academies within or for all of the federation:

> Governors [in the outstanding base school] have agreed to set up an academy trust . . . [and a university] have agreed to be a member of that board of trustees. (Ht 11)

Federation governing bodies usually had strategic committees which worked closely with the head:

> The Chairman's Committee is the strategic committee. (Ht 26)
>
> Strategic governors' committees are very interesting because that is where support and challenge is. (Ht 23)
>
> We have an 18-strong GB as a single governing body with only two committees, so it's much easier. (Ht 25)

For Ht 22 in an academy, and headteachers Ht 23, Ht 25 with a federation, it had been relatively straightforward to reduce the number of governors in all the schools to one governing body. However, Ht 26 also highlighted that a limit for his federation was the number of governors expected by the community:

> You can have fewer governors but that's not the issue. The issue is with so many schools everyone wants to have a part of it. (Ht 26)

This issue had been resolved by Ht 23 by encouraging many of the governors in the schools joining the federation to join parents' groups.

The reduction in the numbers of governors and a more strategic role for them was welcomed; however, it was also acknowledged that more power in the hands of governors could be counter productive but the skill of the head was to manage it:

> Yes, that could be a double edged sword . . .you could have a maverick or rogue among them but your job as head is to get the governors you deserve. (Ht 23)

Relationship with governors in supported schools

Reaction of governors in client schools depended partly on the nature of the involvement of the supporting head as short-term consultant, interim head or overall executive head of multiple schools. Sometimes, governors were aware of the difficulties in their school and just grateful for support. When commenting on the process of being appointed interim headteacher of a second school, one head described the process:

> I went to see the governors, just for five minutes really, and they interviewed me and offered me the job and we went on from there. (Ht 21)

When a school is in special measures and the governors are deemed to have failed, they relinquish a lot of influence and power regarding who is sent in by the LA to lead or support them. Although the school was in special measures, Ht 21 was a well-known face in his community. However, frustration led to governors in some supported schools seeing the system leaders as a threat, particularly if they had been in post and were part of the inadequate judgement:

> When I first went in, the September the reaction was 'Who are you? What's your track record?' They felt very much done to by the LA . . . It was a shame because there were a lot of strengths in the GB . . . However, they didn't meet and hadn't been provided with the right information and so hadn't been supported.' (Ht 24)
>
> They were worried they would lose their head, which they did, and because they didn't understand the fullness of what as going on they thought they were going to lose someone who was very good. (Ht 19)

However, governors new to post, possibly because they were not associated with previous failure, had a different attitude:

> I met with the chair and vice chair of the school. It has happened now three times that when a new chair comes in, they are willing to take the bold step. (Ht 23)
>
> 'Governance in B and C is appalling. It is listed in the SEF as inadequate. However in C they are, with a very good chair, now trying to do something about it and are very well led by the acting head.' (Ht 11)

On one occasion gratitude was expressed by governors to a headteacher for her leading their school to a satisfactory inspection when special measures had been forecast prior to her arrival (Ht 13).

Moving from one governing body in each school to having one overall for the federation can cause some friction with governors in the schools which were going to be absorbed into the federation:

> That was the sticking point and that was the part of what the parents latched on to – their lack of voice. In many schools and even some good schools, the governance is too much embedded in the school. It's wedded to the micro-management of the schools and not to strategic governance. (Ht 23)

Changing partnerships: parents

The importance of headteachers as a presence in schools is linked to their being perceived as the key person responsible for children's progress (Crawford, 2007). However, in terms of new roles for headteachers, the parents had only a minimal impact on the decision to undertake or maintain them. It was acknowledged, nevertheless, that parental reaction had to be considered when heads were working externally or with roles involving structural reform:

> I'm not saying it [federations] couldn't work here but you would have to win hearts and minds of the communities. (Ht 12)

There are sensitive issues to be considered if federations are driven into existence through the failure of one of the schools. Sometimes the expected outcome of long-term collaboration or federation isn't initially clear to all. In these circumstances, the LA and heads tread carefully until all parties, most notably the parents, are informed:

> So we met to talk about how it was going to go forward. It was so cloak and dagger in those days and you couldn't even say the word federation because it had so many connotations. (Ht 23)
>
> I couldn't tell the children and the parents I was head and worked through the deputy. You end up with these bizarre setups because everything has to be done the right way. (Ht 19)

The two issues raised by parents and others during consultation were consistent across the interviews. Parents' concerns were losing the school's identity, and the credibility of the supporting head:

> One of the big fears from parents was that it would be a takeover bid. Some parents thought one site would close and we would develop the other. Another thought both would close with a new build in the middle. (Ht 25)

> The key issue when we were consulting was about credibility. Parents, staff, children and governors wanted a leader who was credible in the community and had the drive and the school at the heart of what they were doing. (Ht 24)

Headteachers identified a risk that when initially undertaking new roles they could lose their good relationships with parents:

> Whether the head is a charismatic leader or not, they have the status of headteacher. Acting headteacher does not have the same status does it? (Ht 11)

Therefore, they constantly monitored the impact of their absence and/or accessibility:

> I would come back here and, although the parents are mostly OK, they didn't like me to be out for two and half days and you get a few ripples here and there. (Ht 8)

> I mean, I can come back to a list of parents moaning . . . I have to manage the fact that I have to come back and deal with things but that is just a fact of life, really. You always carry the mantle of responsibility as a head, regardless. (Ht 18)

Accessibility became an issue for heads of federations. They tried to minimize any negative feelings about their absence by liaising with parents and considering their reactions:

> No, I don't think they [parents] were all that enthusiastic at first, but I make sure I am around for them as much as before if I can, and they see just as much of me, really. (Ht 21)

> At the beginning of my headships, I did nothing but patrol the playgrounds at the start and end of the day so that parents saw that I was around. I wanted to make an impact but they trust I am here now and so I can be in my office doing some work but the open door policy is very strong. (Ht 25)

Heads reported dashing backwards and forwards on the same day to manage schools in the early days of crisis (Ht 20, Ht 25). However, such a way of working could only be short term and heads had to find ways of managing their absence strategically. One way of doing so was to make it obvious their role had changed. Ht 23, for example, moved to a different building on site and the results were that:

> They [parents] changed overnight because their mindset was that I was now the executive head and not the head. (Ht 23)

Apart from initial concerns, heads reported a general lack of criticism from parents, which is possibly because the main criteria for them is the best education for their children. Providing the school and its leadership was validated as successful parents were prepared to trust the governors and heads to make the decision over roles.

Changing Internal Roles and System Leadership 5

This chapter considers the changing role of headteachers and how they have both recognized and responded to the changes they face through opportunity or imposition.

Changing internal roles

Every Child Matters: Children's centres, extended schools and multi-agency work

There is evidence from all the heads in the first two rounds that they knew the ECM agenda would strongly impact on their role and 'is going to be hugely important' (Ht 1), but in the early stages, unless the heads had a children's centre, there was less understanding of how this would be manifested:

> I think ECM is a classic example of people not knowing what is going to happen in schools. (Ht 5)
>
> I have a funny view about all this multi-agency approach . . . I don't think there is a view of what it is going to look like at the moment. (Ht 15)

By round three, unless the heads were describing their children's centre, the ECM agenda wasn't mentioned as an issue. The exception was Ht 25, who believed that due to the nature of the cuts to spending being implemented by the Coalition:

> I decided that this party had lost the plot with every child matters and that to them every child doesn't matter. (Ht 25)

The method of implementation of extended schools and the requirement to include ECM in the new SEF from 2005 was generally disliked, as it was 'imposed' and too 'quickly' (Ht 14). This was seen by some as another part of their undoable role already complicated by too many responsibilities:

> I mean, the job is already unmanageable now and if it grows any more, then you will have to separate the educational leader from the extended school leader . . . I don't think we could do it all at the same time. (Ht 15)

However there was also acknowledgement that:

> ECM is the best thing to come out of the [Education] Department . . . We have stopped talking about a child just in school and started to look at whole people. (Ht 5)

Heads whose role had changed due to ECM with co-location of mainstream schools with special schools (Ht 3), or the heads with existing or prospective children's centres, while finding the disruption and even the initial imposition of the centre difficult were all prepared to tolerate the situation because it was seen to benefit the community:

> I never applied to become a children's centre but I got a letter saying 'congratulations on your application'! My first reaction was like I am usually, which is to say 'great – something new, here's a challenge' that sort of thing and that's the way I work. (Ht 13)

Three heads strived for a centre but had not yet been able to achieve it and were frustrated at the delay or postponement. Their anger was directed at the LA because, despite planning and commitment, the money had not been found from grants to pay for it (Ht 4, Ht 5), or there was general inefficiency regarding the process summed up by this comment:

> They [LA] said to me in the middle of March – 'Can you spend this money by the end of the year?' So I did. We have got all the furniture for it, but they haven't put a spade in the ground. In fact, they haven't even got planning permission yet, which is silly. (Ht 16)

The ECM agenda changed heads' roles due to an increased workload, particularly for those involved in children's centres and extended schools. Although children's centre managers were employed by governors in centres attached to schools, this usually came later and the initial setup and integration into the school system often fell to the headteacher:

> It's almost like another school being amalgamated with us and all the emotional stress that goes with that and the amount of staff that are involved . . . It took so much energy last year – it was unbelievable. (Ht 19)

A consequence of the introduction of ECM was the increased responsibility for LAs with the introduction of children's services. None of the heads rated the services of multi-agency support. There were complaints about the bureaucracy and work overload involved in working with other agencies and pessimism over future relationships as typified by this comment:

> but social services never really work together with anybody, so how is that going to work? I have never known anyone as poor at communicating as they are, so what will happen there? (Ht 11)

Sure Start was singled out for its ineffectiveness:

> Sure Start is such a bloody bureaucracy . . . The task groups meet regularly but nobody actually does anything – it's just talk! (Ht 5)
>
> Our children's centre has had to take over all the Sure Start work . . . The government wanted it in schools and integrated because they don't think Sure Start is doing it properly and it doesn't take rocket science to work that out. (Ht 19)

It was never the intention that heads would both manage children's centres and schools together. There was the expectation that the children's centre would be managed, but this person would not have to be a teacher let alone the headteacher. However the situation is complicated by accountability. Heads were concerned that if they were accountable for the school then to what extent were they also accountable for the children's centre? (See Chapter 6.)

Some heads hoped that the ECM agenda and closer multi-agency working would improve issues around 'the assessment for inclusion' (Ht 8), although the increased workload around this was also recognised:

> I think the whole inclusion agenda has had a big impact on issues for heads. That's another lot of time consuming forms . . . the whole Crisping, the audit, it's a massive agenda. (Ht 14)

'Crisping' children is the use of the CRISP audit profile to identify the need for resources for children with special needs.

The bureaucracy was worse for two small school heads (Ht 9, Ht 25), who had to undertake the role of inclusion leader themselves.

Extended schools provision for clubs and activities out of school hours was generally well received because of the anticipated benefits to the school's community. However, it also created more work for heads, and the role was quickly delegated:

> We have got an out of school hours club but it is actually run separate to school and that's how we want it to stay at least for the time being – we've got enough. (Ht 15)

Other new models of school leadership in a single institution

Only one headteacher (Ht 15) was involved in co-headship for 50 per cent of each week. She chose co-leadership with another, as both wanted the role part-time to pursue an external role and for personal commitments and not as an exit strategy for retirement. Another new model of school leadership was the co-location of a special school on the site of Ht 3's primary school. At the time of the first interview it was in the planning stage, having been suggested by the head of a local special school, with the aim of making the one organization 'inclusive'. By the time of the revisit for the second round, the building work was in progress and the school was 'undergoing a total rebuild' (Ht 3). It impacted greatly on the role of the headteachers of both the primary school and the head of the special school, but it was considered worth it at the time because of the benefits to the community.

Leaders of education: national and local

In 2010, there were 393 NLEs from all phases (NC, 2011a), increased from 68 in October 2006 (Hill and Matthews, 2008) and this pattern was echoed in the research. By May 2011, 14 of the heads had been or were NLEs, whereas only four of them were NLEs in 2006. One head (Ht 19) had moved school and no longer fitted the NLE criteria in round three. While doing similar work, she was not leading an outstanding school while doing so. This is a high percentage, as NLE status was not a requirement of the sample. Most heads had shown interest in system leadership previously as consultant leaders. It could therefore be expected that they would have an interest in the latest opportunities.

From experience, I am aware that it was the practice for some heads to deploy staff from their schools to support in other schools before the introduction of National Leaders of Education and National Support Schools (NLENSS). However it is an *expectation* for NLEs to use their staff when supporting schools. There was agreement regarding the purpose of the role encapsulated by this comment:

> I strongly believe that the NLE model came from the fact that the department wanted to get around local authorities where local authorities are not effective and I have no doubt and there is no question in my mind about that. I think they have been extremely unhelpful in not being honest. (Ht 20)

Heads were keen to explain that the role of NLE was a privilege and that they didn't use it as a status symbol:

> Apart from it giving me some credibility in the schools I am supporting, if they know I am an NLE, it stops silly questions being asked, but other than that I don't use it. (Ht 26)

The reasons for the decision to apply for NLE status were given as moral purpose, increasing credibility and invitation:

> I think applying for NLE is also the way forward for our two schools and also for recruitment where we can say we have the best teachers and best leaders. (Ht 24)

> Following that experience [successful executive leadership] I became an NLE and this school is a National Support School (NSS). So it was a natural follow on from that recognition, I guess. (Ht 26)

> The LA asked me to apply to become an NLE in 2008 because of our work supporting another school. (Ht 13)

Work was mainly brokered by the LAs. It was usually their decision how NLEs were deployed and there were differences in practice, which sometimes changed over time. Ht 13 felt that her LA 'had no plan' for what to do in a crisis where schools were failing and was relying on NLEs to help them. She reiterated the comments of Ht 20 that because LAs haven't shown they can tackle the job, heads are being brought in to do so. Support for this view from an NLE whose involvement with the strategic role of the LA increased as the role of her NSS decreased:

> However, I think the role is changing somewhat . . . I am being invited more and more to be part of management review teams for the LA. (Ht 14)

Although this head was working to support a vulnerable school, she was also being used to fill a capacity gap in the LA and believed this was a less effective way to support schools:

> I definitely think it is better to work as before for me, and us, here as an independent NLE. That is because the package we brokered with the school let us determine the support. (Ht 14)

Ht 22 was not deployed by her LA for school-to-school support because, 'The LA refuses to use us', as she led an academy. However, unlike Ht 14, she wouldn't work as a surrogate adviser and was unequivocal in her definition of what the role should be:

> My role as an NLE isn't to support an unsatisfactory headteacher who has got the school in a mess and didn't see it coming. I want the role to be much more strategic than that and not providing a sticking plaster. (Ht 22)

Seven heads incorporated the supported school/s into their federations or collaborations rather than act as consultants. However, some NLEs preferred to work in short-term collaborations:

> I would prefer to go in with an exit strategy to come away with. I don't want to be the head of another school. (Ht 14)

While recognising support depended on context:

> [we] help the schools move from our intensive support to less, and then coaching and mentoring and interim strategies before exiting leaving them stronger. It depends on them having the people that can do that . . . However there are other schools where the SLT aren't capable and so then there needs to be something like a federation because improvement won't then be sustained with the model of the support school walking away. (Ht 14)

All heads believed the role had longevity. Many saw their role as being used as a 'network of support' (27) following the identification of issues by the LA or OFSTED:

> A local adviser working along side the NLE or LLE will write an action plan and I guess have termly meetings to determine the progress. (Ht 27)

How heads built capacity to undertake these roles is considered in Chapter 7.

Changing school structures

Free schools

The Coalition government introduced a system of free schools due to open from September 2011. This was too late for heads to comment on their impact on the system for this book. Nevertheless, heads expressed their opinions regarding the implications of free schools for the future role of headship. Some heads were sceptical:

> I don't know much about them, but they haven't raised standards in Sweden, have they? Just think it fits in with Tory philosophy. (Ht 19)

One head was broadly positive with the belief that those who set up free schools did so 'with the right motives . . . because they want good outcomes for children' (Ht 11). Others were 'worried' over the apparent freedoms they would enjoy:

> You are allowed to have unqualified teachers in free schools, which is undermining our professionalism again. (Ht 25)

> But my interpretation of them here is that you can set up anything even like an atheist anti-establishment type of school and there is no one that will stop you and I think that could be dangerous. (Ht 22)

Ht 11 believed that 'in time' the heads of free schools would work alongside those of non-independent state schools because 'most headteachers want to collaborate', but acknowledged that this would:

> to some extent depend on whether they are fighting for pupil numbers that might make a difference. (Ht 11)

There was a view, too, that there would be very few created:

> I actually think there are going to be very few free schools. I may be completely wrong about that but it is almost easier to take a camel through the eye of a needle than to open a free school. The government is interested in them and you might see 100 open over a period of about five years, but that is a small number. (Ht 27)

Those which were created would be likely to succeed because they had the strong backing of the government:

> I think there will be free schools which will succeed because the Department and the Secretary of State will need some to succeed and so, therefore, if you are at the beginning and at the cutting edge, those schools will get every single support mechanism and support structure to ensure that they do succeed. (Ht 20)

Academies

Following the change of government in 2010, outstanding heads had the opportunity to convert to academy status. The definition of academy used in this section is that defined by the Coalition, as opposed to those created for secondary schools under the previous Labour government. There was recognition of the differences between the 'old' style academies of the Labour government and the 'new' academies being introduced from September 2010:

> They aren't about government picking up weak schools but about strong schools. I know they are supposed to support weak schools but there is support and support. (Ht 13)

While government was pleased to have conversion in a variety of formats, the new academies didn't need to involve sponsors. Many heads rejected firmly the prospect of losing their autonomy to a chain of providers:

> We don't want to jump out of bed with the LA and then find we are in a different bed and told we have to do this or that in a particular way . . . There is a certain amount of freedom which would have been lost if we had to become part of an existing chain. (Ht 11)

> I think if you are part of an academy chain those strategic things around funding and development and around staffing structures and high level personnel issues and performance management, and deciding on school improvement priorities, I think decisions around these areas will probably be done by an academy trust, and as an academy head you will be delivering it. (Ht 27)

Becoming an academy was of particular interest to headteachers who were proactive in seeking to shape their future role. Sometimes, this meant they would act quickly to take advantage of opportunities, such as Ht 22, whose school had converted in September 2010, and others (Ht 11, Ht 23, Ht 26) who were actively engaged in the process:

> I am interested but only because I think you need to be in charge of your own destiny. It was plainly obvious from a meeting I was at that the government wants every school to become an academy. So I would rather go now and be in charge of it than go in three years time and someone tell me what kind of a structure I am going to be in. (Ht 23)

Alternatively, others were unsure of the benefits to their school and adopted a wait and see approach:

> I want to know about what's happening to the SATs and the whole area of the curriculum . . . before we start launching off on our own. (Ht 14)

> But, I don't think we are brave enough at the moment and are just watching the national picture. (Ht 24)

> There is no advantage at the moment in becoming an academy school, because the detail hasn't been worked through or developed enough. (Ht 20)

Only one head was ideologically opposed to academies:

> I am completely anti-academy status and it is a political stance. I think academy status will undermine LAs and is privatization by the back door. (Ht 25)

The perceived advantages of academy status were identified as greater freedom, bigger budgets and, above all, a lack of bureaucracy involved with being in an LA, irrespective of the services they used as these examples illustrate:

> I knew constantly that every conversation I was having with the LA, was causing stress, more work, and couldn't carry on much longer. (Ht 22)
>
> People say we should support the LA but, sadly, our LA has failed to provide services . . . The LA are jobsworths and so part of the reason we want to leave is that there isn't any capacity within the LA. (Ht 11)

Heads had a pragmatic attitude towards being forced by circumstances to convert:

> However, if we came to the point where the only source of funding was through academies, I would then have to seriously think about it. (Ht 13)
>
> I think there will be a tipping point because of the demise of the LA. (Ht 20)
>
> I can see, unfortunately, that if enough schools take on academy status we will all be forced down the same way because LA s will crumble. The backing will just disappear. (Ht 25)

Reasons decisions were made about academy conversion are linked to the loyalty heads felt about the schools they supported. Ht 11, who would have been ready sooner as a standalone outstanding school, wouldn't go until all the schools he supported could join 'as a family'. Ht 26 had a complex federation structure and some of the schools in the federation could easily convert. Nevertheless, no one would until all the schools could be involved and he wouldn't convert at all if it meant the break up of the federation.

The government was moving quickly in 2010 to facilitate the creation of academies. Consequently, it was feeling its way regarding the practicalities of the process of implementation:

> The DfE weren't really very hot on the articles and memoranda . . . We were writing the policies and procedures as we needed them. I was constantly onto the DfE for clarification. (Ht 22)
>
> We have applied to become academies but we have made it clear in the application that it would share a single academy trust. So the academies

would be federated with each other by the virtue of the trust and the same governance . . . I think we probably are [unique] and that is probably why the department can't make up its mind. (Ht 26)

For those who were converting or had converted, there was agreement that it was work-intensive in the short term and Ht 22 had spent all of the summer holidays preparing for it, despite using a management company, 'because with them came a legal team for the legal side of it' (Ht 22).

Change to the governance of schools was an integral feature of conversion to academy status. However, it is important here to note that when schools converted, the structure of governance changed from that of other state-maintained schools. This had interesting implications:

The government is either very, very clever or it has found itself in a fortuitous position . . . under academy law you only need about four or five governors. The stakeholder model has been completely swept away. I think the government wanted to do that but didn't want to alienate a vast number of the voluntary sector. By schools changing to become an academy, they have changed governance by the back door. (Ht 23).

Academies were required to work with 'failing' schools and most schools already were as part of their role as NLEs or executive headteachers. It was anticipated that this role would continue or be extended:

Instead of looking at long-term school support, if a school goes into special measures they will look at it becoming part of an academy chain or federate it. That will be the first thing and not the last solution. (Ht 27)

It was a point of speculation as to where the link with failing schools would come from if the relationship with LAs had been broken. Ht 22 highlighted that her LA wouldn't use her school to support others and had 'actually put in writing' that it was 'because you are now an academy' (Ht 22). There is some evidence that the attitude of the LAs to conversion was mixed. Ht 24 suggested:

I think the LA would support us. Those of us in outstanding schools had a meeting with the LA very quickly. They just wanted to say we are here and supporting you. (Ht 24)

There was a potential to change the working conditions of those who work in academies. Initially, the pay and conditions of staff are transferred to the academy but, later, governing bodies could change them. All heads were aware of this and one noted:

> But whatever you take into the academy you can change. So I think people will start with the blue book [pay and conditions document for state schools] and then afterwards start to think what else they can do with it. (Ht 23)

Ht 22 suggested that this was unlikely, as why would a head want to upset the most important resource they had – the staff? Nevertheless, there was the potential to change (see Chapter 7).

Federations and collaborations

There was an increasing understanding of, and interest in, new school structures as they developed throughout the research. Executive heads and the head of an academy reported being invited to conferences and meetings or to participate in research at the request of the National College, DfE or other heads and their governors:

> I have had about 12 phone calls from outstanding and good schools from our LA who are now seriously looking at becoming an academy. They have asked me to talk to their governing bodies and tell them what it really looks like. (Ht 22)

> I have a head and chair coming to see me tomorrow who want to join as part of the family of schools. (Ht 11)

In the first two rounds of interviews, there was much use of the terms 'hard' and 'soft' federation, which is reflected in this section. Hard federation was defined as having one governing body for two or more schools. Soft federations were a strong collaboration involving shared governors' committees, a loose collaboration involved leadership but not governance. By round three, a federation was only being defined by heads as a group of schools with one governing body, with other models deemed collaboration. This can be illustrated clearly by Ht 20, who referred to a federation in 2007 but by 2010 had changed terms for the same two-school model:

> Just to clear up in terms of federation there is no federation between the two schools and neither governing body would see this as a federation. (Ht 20)

There were a variety of formats of school-to-school support which ranged from NLE consultancy in schools with existing heads to leadership of a formal collaboration or federation of schools. Sometimes, for three of the four heads re-interviewed from the second round, both the schools and roles had changed (Ht 11, Ht 14, Ht 19) but not their involvement in system leadership.

The organizations were of between two to five schools, but different in terms of structure and how they were developed. The reasons given for joining together were:

A small school federation due to the viability of the schools

A mixed federation of phases due to existing collaboration arrangements being unsatisfactory

Outstanding or good schools seeking federation benefits

Outstanding school linked with a failing school/s

An outstanding head engaged to lead two vulnerable schools

The structure of the organizations wasn't static. In many cases, they changed, either substituting one school for another, or growing in terms of the number of schools which joined. The benefits of system leadership were such that schools which were failing or in category when they joined were quickly moved on and, in two cases, also became outstanding. Success meant that all the heads were open to the idea of growth. They commented that they would take on new schools but had provisos around their capacity to sustain improvement or the type of school they would consider:

Our schools would have the capacity at the moment to take another school into the group if we thought that was the right thing to do. We would only be interested in a failing school of course. (Ht 20)

I would definitely take on another school in a federation . . . I would still be interested, provided that I could be assured we could do it. (Ht 13)

The optimum number of schools in a federation depended on the leadership role heads would undertake themselves and is considered in detail in Chapter 7.

Some federations in the system are cross-phase, including that of Ht 26. There was a mixed response to the benefits of this structure:

They [secondary schools] are going to go for academy status and they are going to mop up all the local primaries that feed into them especially in the shires where

> there is a very distinct feeder school system . . . I am massively opposed to that
> and so I am looking . . . to make a purely primary system of academies across 10
> schools. (Ht 23)

> I think there might be more primary and secondary federations . . . It's good for
> the system . . . A children's centre through to 19 could be a very viable proposition
> and I would be interested in that. (Ht 24)

> I am really interested in them [cross-phase federations] . . . I think people's interest
> often depends on whether they are going to be the change agent or not. (Ht 19)

Several heads had an issue with 'empire builders . . .on the national scene who
are dominating the agenda at the moment' (Ht 24) or who didn't wish to be
seen as one:

> It concerns me that I would be seen as just an empire builder and I don't like that
> image, especially with other heads. You have to be modest about it. (Ht 13)

There were different drivers behind structural reform. Mainly, the LAs initially brokered the support of the headteachers to take over the leadership of
a failing school/s:

> It is a soft collaboration between the three schools . . . The LA saw it as having a
> more experienced mentor working alongside . . . I suppose I am the glue between
> the three schools in terms of working with the heads. (Ht 11)

> At the moment . . . , you are a strong school and the other is a weak one and I can
> see why it's like that, but shouldn't be always . . . they could come in at a more
> equal level. (Ht 13)

Headteachers had firstly made the LA aware that they were seeking this type
of external role:

> We had been through a second really good OFSTED here and we felt secure and
> that we had the capacity to be able to run another school. So we offered to be a
> pilot or flagship or whatever they wanted to call it for the LA if they found another
> school. (Ht 23)

In one situation, two headteachers rated by OFSTED as outstanding made the
initial decision to federate:

> The schools . . . became part of a schools' trust, but it didn't do what it said
> on the tin. So there wasn't a real accountability model within that . . . So this

school and [another] decided that we thought we should look at federation.
(Ht 26)

Once in existence, the expansion of the groups was a combination of factors which included the system leaders' approach to other heads, the heads of schools wishing to become part of a federation, or the LA requesting that other vulnerable schools join. For example, Ht 23 had a federation which started as an average-sized successful primary school, and was invited by the LA to work with a small vulnerable neighbour, and another, and then expanded to include other good schools whose heads had chosen to join. Similarly, the federation of Ht 26 expanded from a federation between two outstanding schools to become three successful schools and then again to include a vulnerable school. Having started initially as collaborations brokered through the LA, some schools were driven to become federations by the system leaders concerned as these heads noted:

> I was pushing for hard federation . . . I was having six to ten meetings every half term. It was becoming crazy and I said to governors that it needed to change. (Ht 25)

> We created what was deemed a collaboration . . . That was a termed agreement . . . [Later] I started to talk about my future . . . and that I was looking elsewhere. The LA and the GB started to talk about a longer term solution and we started to explore federation. (Ht 24)

As more schools federated or collaborated, the concept of chains of schools became an issue which heads felt they needed to consider. The idea of having a brand within a group or group of federated primary or lower and middle schools was discussed:

> When the chair and I looked at how we would run a federation, we were deliberately looking at five schools as a minimum or five to eight schools. So, every structure we put in would work for five to eight schools and not just two schools. Where people have fallen down is where they have just treated federation as a done deal. Often they don't get rid of, or rethink, old systems and structures. (Ht 23)

> The idea is to create a chain of four or five schools over a two-year period and brand them with my current school branding. (Ht 27)

An addition to the debate of branding schools is the likelihood of selling this brand as a school improvement package. In this way, individual heads of federations could be setting up as providers to rival sponsorship chains:

> If you have a school with a good standard operating model and procedures, can you replicate that and give other young people high standards and a great educational experience. (Ht 20)

The replication of systems or leadership practice across federations is discussed in Chapter 7.

School chains were sponsored by organizations such as Ark Schools, an educational charity, Oasis Community Learning group or the Harris Academies set up by Lord Harris Chairman and Chief Executive of Carpetright plc, none of which were represented in the sample. However, Ht 11 had been approached and had refused. His refusal was based on his concern that he would lose his autonomy, a view endorsed by others:

> There is an issue about academy chains for the role of the headteacher in chains is vastly reduced because it has a trust over it. The trust makes the major decisions about the school and the funding. The headteacher in chains is more like a head of school. (Ht 27)

There was an assumption by the interviewees that as they were successful, if they worked with other schools, it would be on their terms. It didn't occur to any of them that a head from outside might in some way be imposed upon them by a sponsor, governors or the LA.

The future: networks and teaching schools

Networks

Networks of federations or collaborations were highlighted as being an important development for the future. Formal arrangements were considered to be more effective than loose collaborations, because of commitment and the accountability of the members:

> You only need one person to procrastinate, miss a meeting and it completely collapses. So, while you might get the majority at the table, it only takes one not to be there and it just doesn't work. (Ht 26)

Reasons given for networking were given as economies of scale and spreading best practice to avoid other schools failing:

> There will be more partnerships and collaborations and federations . . . I think we will have collaborations between schools being made driven by financial need rather than purely the need of children. (Ht 24)

> In terms of do I think schools should belong to a network of schools and challenge and be part of the development of improvement within the schools in that network, then yes, I do. Do I think all schools will end up in a chain or a federation, then no, I don't. I think it will be used according to how the LA and the department think schools can best be served when they are failing. (Ht 27)

The role of the LA was an important factor in the growth of networks. There was a general consensus that the LA was going to change radically following the changes made by the Coalition in 2010, particularly regarding cuts to their budgets. One head noted, 'I think it will be a total disaster for them' (Ht 13), and another that 'it will crush the LA if too many schools become an academy' (Ht 25). There was mixed sympathy for the LAs regarding their uncertain future:

> The problem I've had is with the capacity of the LA. People say we should support the LA but, sadly, our LA has failed to provide services, with the exception of one or two things, and I think schools and heads working collaboratively can get better services. They just have never got the message. (Ht 11)

There was a consensus that the LA had no strategic vision for its future:

> The LA is having to deal with cuts and the government, but they don't think far enough ahead. We are talking about the commissioning of services for the city, but I don't think until we have the strategic view of what the future will look like for our city that we are in a position to know what partnerships and services we will need. (Ht 24)

> We should be asking, 'Where are the models and what do they look like?' . . . and they [the LA] should say, 'Lets look nationally and internationally and go and see some new models and come back and decide what does it mean for our city and how can we learn from it?' (Ht 13)

Due to the lack of capacity in LAs, heads perceived that it would be difficult for them to identify failure due to a lack of 'local intelligence' deemed essential to broker system leadership (Higham, Hopkins and Matthews, 2009):

> The LA doesn't necessarily know where the need is and I think that is going to become increasingly difficult for me and others who do these roles because there is a lack of understanding and support for it. (Ht 24)

Assuming LAs could identify failure, then schools working together were viewed as being able to take on some of the role of the LA in terms of school improvement:

> I think satisfactory schools will be driven to it [federation] because the LAs will all have imploded by then. (Ht 22)
>
> We will have to pick up the leadership function of the LA. We have great teams in schools and I am sure we can share to pick that up and for CPD. We have enough skills to manage all that. (Ht 13)

There was also a widespread view that some heads who were not as experienced or deemed as effective would struggle without LA support, at least until networks or clusters could take over the role. This was highlighted by several heads as typified by these examples:

> I think the LA blocks the impact schools can have and ours is very paternal and deskills the heads. I know heads who say, 'That's the LAs' responsibility', and I say, 'Why? You are the paid professional so you make the decision.' (Ht 23)
>
> I suspect the smaller schools because of the nature of the leadership require the comfort of the LA network in a different way to a larger institution. So I can almost imagine a LA for primaries with all the secondaries moving away. (Ht 26)

Another head agreed that the more heads used the LAs the more difficult it would be if its provision declined:

> The LA is going to be greatly reduced and the more we use it, the greater the difficulty when it is reduced. It is actually quite frightening and where are you going to go for support from agencies? I had it priced up recently and an educational psychiatrist is £300 per hour. I can't afford that with a budget which is 98 per cent staffing and the rest is learning and resources. What are we going to do for this support if the LAs go under? (Ht 25)

It was speculated upon that as their capacity diminished, the LAs would engage NLEs and LLEs more frequently and take advantage of the increasing numbers being made available by government policy (DfE, 2010). It was believed that NLEs would lead networks possibly, but not exclusively, as leaders of teaching schools as the hub of a network.

Teaching schools

Teaching schools were announced in the white paper (DfE, 2010b). The TES (Dec 2010) suggested that most leaders preferred teacher training to be delivered by universities. Contrastingly, the development was very popular with interviewees who speculated about their potential role in leading one:

> We would have a much stronger influence around teacher training and this would have a good impact on recruitment. (Ht 11)

> If we want to train NQTs, for example, we can send them to each other's schools and we do that now but we would have to formalize that a little bit more. We can easily manage that and I really like the idea of setting up our own teacher training. (Ht 13)

There were some comments about the likely importance of networks of schools with a teaching school as the lead, providing or sourcing training for leadership of staff in the locality. An issue highlighted by heads for any form of voluntary collaboration was to what extent would schools want to do so?

> Yes, but how are they going to persuade some schools to work in partnership with others? Some schools just like to work in isolation for what they can get for themselves. A lot of heads don't see the value of partnership in terms of giving for the greater good. They don't mind receiving but it is important that there is a lot of give and take. (Ht 13)

Generally, however, heads were optimistic regarding the development of networks of support:

> I would hope that leaders would naturally form networks . . . [but] . . . I don't think any school should be allowed not to be in a partnership. (Ht 23)

> I am very optimistic about that. It is what I want to see. That is my vision for school improvement . . . I see absolutely no reason why the conurbations around the country shouldn't be in networks where everyone supports one another. The main strand of school improvement is rooted in schools. (Ht 27)

Heads recognized the importance of building capacity in schools to manage new roles. While doing so, they needed to consider the impact of standards of attainment and their accountability for the performance of their school or schools.

Standards, Accountability and Leadership 6

Many new roles have developed for headteachers because of a form of credibility they have attained, or earned autonomy granted through validation from successful inspections. Pivotal to the success of these were high standards achieved and/or attained. It is not surprising, therefore, that most of the issues impacting on the role of the heads as they identified them were described either in relation to their impact on, or how they were affected by, the relentless drive for standards and in order for the heads to satisfy the various forms of accountability for which they were subject. This chapter considers the impact on the role of primary headteachers of standards and accountability for performance of themselves and of their schools.

The relentless drive for standards

The emphasis on standards has had a major impact on the role of headteachers during the last 15 years. While the degree of stress it generated was of varying degrees, there was no distinction as far as the importance of standards was concerned in terms of the timing of the interviews or the context of the schools.

Heads of small schools in both urban and rural contexts commented:

> Standards are definitely our biggest pressure because of OFSTED. I don't think there is anything else. (Ht 9)

> The pressure for me is the SATs and there's no denying we have to make sure that those are good . . . If I wake up thinking about anything, then it's that. (Ht 21)

Heads from large urban two- or three-form entry schools stated:

> Well, it has to be standards . . . It occupies most of my time and role as a head. (Ht 18)

> With the present system, the end of key stage results have to be the highest on the agenda for accountability and, of course, OFSTED. (Ht 14)

> The pressures of getting our sort of children to the expected levels are phenomenal. (Ht 19)

> It impacts highly on me and is very significant in all the schools I work in. I do feel very pressured for standards. (Ht 27)

The pressure to raise standards in one or more schools, from the point of view of achieving the highest possible SATs scores, impacts on other aspects of how headteachers lead schools. These areas include curriculum design and assessment, inclusion and the management of the accountability process through inspection by OFSTED.

Standards and the curriculum

The majority of the heads' responses indicated that their perceived need to maximise test results had impacted on the structure and delivery of the curriculum:

> I know how to organize the teaching and learning for them [the children] to get optimum standards. (Ht 13)

> Particularly because [the client] school was in a category, only one aspect really mattered and that is literacy, numeracy and science, and so we worked heavily on that. (Ht 19)

Towards the end of the Labour government, the influence of The National Strategies for Literacy and Numeracy was residual as they were due to cease in March 2011, a policy decision confirmed by the Coalition.

However, when they were introduced, they had considerable impact on the curriculum. There has been widespread criticism of them and their impact on pedagogy, creativity and the wider curriculum (Docking, 2000; Alexander. 2010), and there was some sympathy with this view from everyone, as illustrated below:

> The literacy hour – what a nonsense! Two minutes for this and ten minutes for that . . . It was just a farce. (Ht 25)

It was also acknowledged by a minority (Ht 2, Ht 4, Ht 15) that the National Strategies helped them to raise standards, perhaps because it offered a 'life-belt' (Ht 4), as teachers knew what they had to teach to cover what would be tested:

> The great thing about the Strategy is that it gives you a systematic approach to teaching literacy and numeracy which we didn't have. (Ht 15)

The strategies were never mandatory but they were so effectively marketed by the Labour government, this fact is almost irrelevant. Many heads either didn't realize they had a choice or implemented them through fear of the consequences of school failure being associated by the LAs and particularly OFSTED with non-compliance.

After the strategies had been in place for some years, schools had to be strongly encouraged to teach creatively and to 'personalize' learning (Miliband, 2004), as the government had become worried that standards had plateaued in their second term. The plateauing of standards being a reason for change was recognized by the interviewees, as this head noted when commenting on why schools were being encouraged to consider a more creative curriculum from 2005:

> Because it hasn't worked. No good hitting a plateau. We know it's about standards and that's all they care about. (Ht 2)

Nevertheless, the majority of heads resisted a purely standards-driven curriculum and attempted to balance this with ensuring that the curriculum was creative and interesting for children. Balance and context are important in this debate. Headteachers in good to outstanding schools are more likely to have the autonomy from the LA or OFSTED to determine the direction of the curriculum. However, this in itself brings the pressure to maintain their position and the temptation to teach to the test to do so:

> People definitely have to teach to the test of course they do . . . Most schools have to, so we can be sure of the results. (Ht 16)
>
> I think any teaching to the test is inevitable but it has to be limited and you have to be sensible about it and unfortunately a lot of our colleagues aren't. One would be naïve to think there won't be some teaching to the test. (Ht 27)

There was considerable enthusiasm for the findings of the Rose Review (2009) of the curriculum agreed by the Labour government to be implemented from September 2011. It was opposed in Parliament by the Conservatives while in opposition in April 2010 and shelved by the incoming Coalition the following May. This was greeted with general disappointment, as typified by this head:

> When we got a letter about the Rose Review and then the letter about the cuts, I hope I was one of many who clicked the button and replied [to the DfE] saying 'Prove to me why it wouldn't work and why adding 36 learning skills to the curriculum wouldn't enhance children's learning.' (Ht 25)

Standards and assessment

Every year group needs to perform to achieve optimum standards for the school. Data needs to be collated and evaluated to identify any dips in performance for individual cohorts or children. Nearly all the heads described the importance of a 'water-tight tracking system and assessment program' (Ht 14), and analyzing the data produced to enable them to show the children's progress and gain a good result from OFSTED. Many headteachers kept a very close eye on children's ongoing assessments, sometimes to the extent of tracking or identifying trends themselves:

> I coordinate the assessment. I spend a lot of time on it because I want it done properly and I like to be able to track every child and look and see the trends. (Ht 18)

> I think you need to be good at data analysis as a head and you have got to have a
> rigorous system . . . and identify where the gaps are and where you need to make
> the improvements. (Ht 17)

This level of operational control is more difficult for executive heads; nevertheless, they created systems to overcome this:

> I have had to accept that I no longer know every single child but as we have sharp-
> ened assessments I have a much better understanding. If someone asks me about
> a particular child, all I have to do is open a particular file. (Ht 13)

The curriculum also had to be adapted and reviewed to ensure that it targeted improvement:

> We are also looking at the curriculum with regard to making it more focused,
> particularly on maths and analyzing where the children are falling down. (Ht 10)

> Standards started to dramatically go up and then over the last couple of years the
> writing SATs changed and that's where they found it hard . . . so within the school
> now, our big issue is writing. (Ht 8)

In 2010, the issues around the unfairness of SATs testing came to a head when the National Association of Headteachers (NAHT) balloted headteachers, recommending that they boycott the tests. There was a mixed reaction to this request. While most heads believed SATs were to varying degrees ineffective, this didn't always translate into avoidance in 2010:

> I didn't boycott the tests. Everyone had worked really hard for them, children par-
> ticularly, and staff and the tests have never done us any harm here. (Ht 14)

> If we had known there weren't going to be any SATs a year beforehand, then I
> may not have done them. Once it got to January and they had worked their hearts
> out to do their best, then I wasn't going to stop that and the teachers didn't want
> to. (Ht 27)

It was suggested that there was some degree of peer pressure to boycott the tests from other heads and local school networks, which may have influenced the decisions of some. Ht 13 reported that her chair of governors was vehemently opposed to the school undertaking the tests. Others were aware of 'very strong feelings about boycotting them' (Ht 14) in consortium meetings.

Standards and Every Child Matters

Heads believed that the ECM agenda was already embedded into schools and wouldn't require much change to the curriculum or impact detrimentally on standards:

> Once I realized that it was pretty much the same, just in five categories, I didn't worry about it. (Ht 17)

> We have got the ECM agenda. We have got to see how it can work concurrently alongside what we are already doing in the curriculum. We are already doing a lot, but it's just recognizing it. (Ht 10)

While adapting the curriculum to accommodate ECM was welcomed, there was a tension between maximizing results and inclusion of children, regardless of any special need:

> The trouble is that the government want it all and don't know how to get it . . . They want all children to be average and so they don't understand what averages are, therefore. You can't have everybody average, can you! (Ht 16)

The needs of children who experience environmental poverty were highlighted by many as challenges to improving SATs standards, particularly around the poor behaviour of some children:

> The challenge is in inner city schools, where you have got both agendas of ECM and standards pushing at both levels – that's where it is hard. (Ht 9)

> Because we have got some very difficult kids we work on it . . . This is what is so difficult when people like OFSTED come in. They see these well-behaved kids and they think they should be achieving even more – they don't realize how difficult it is to get them to this point. I find it's a massive pressure. (Ht 11)

Accountability of the headteacher and autonomy

Headteachers welcomed their professional duty to ensure children's entitlement to care and a good education and for parents to be satisfied with the school's provision for their children. However, it was believed accountability was very strong partly because of a lack of trust in the profession:

> It is certainly about lack of trust. Certainly we are the least trusted of all professions. The fact is that Harold Shipman can do away with 300 people and we have to check that someone hasn't bought their wife a dishwasher out of petty cash. (Ht 5)

> Doctors do not have a government person looking over their shoulders telling them how to cure a patient's cancer. (Ht 25)

Accountability and OFSTED

Following the introduction of OFSTED in 1992 being held to account for the performance of their schools is the main form of accountability for heads and impacted strongly on their role. Whether or not it was manifested through inspection by OFSTED, heads accepted that some form of external accountability for schools was necessary:

> There have to be ways of judging schools. I don't think you can go back to how it used to be. (Ht 16)

> Well I don't welcome it [OFSTED], but the bottom line is that not everybody does the same high quality job, do they? (Ht 5)

> I have been picking up the pieces for some years and there are weak heads and there needs to be accountability. (Ht 19)

However, they were all concerned about the fairness and consistency of the process of accountability for the performance of schools, both at individual school and system level:

> I have no problem with OFSTED as the idea of external assessment, but it has always been a deficit model and not a model for school improvement . . . It is the range of abilities of the people who are inspectors. It just isn't consistently good. (Ht 23)

Headteachers were well aware of the need to prepare for OFSTED inspection. They were aware of the impact it would have on their professional reputation and how they were perceived as leaders, and so described their issues in terms of it. These form the basis of the next subheadings:

> Data and inspection
> School self evaluation

SIPs and LAs

Stress and inspection

New roles and new accountabilities

Data and inspection

The amount of data held on schools has increased massively throughout the years, as the government encouraged informed professionalism where 'teachers are driven by data and what the data tells them' (Barber, 2002, 187). This showed no signs of abating with a change of government in 2010. When headteachers described the impact of inspection on their roles, they highlighted the importance of data to the inspection process:

> There is a strong link between data and the outcome of inspections and I think it will only get stronger as we will be soon inspected only on the back of what your data looks like. (Ht 27)
>
> I worry in that I want to show both schools in the best light . . . I know that the inspectors are driven by data and outcomes. (Ht 24)

With only one or two days notice for inspection, there was little time for inspectors to concentrate on issues other than standards. This exacerbated the pressure to show results:

> Let's put it this way, when the data is high, they [inspectors] have time to look at other aspects . . . But when the data is low, they go for the jugular straight away. (Ht 19)

The impact of deprivation on the outcome of standards was recognised by the Labour government with the inclusion of a measurement of progress or a value-added factor from KS1–KS2 as well as attainment data. The framework for inspection was differentiated in that both attainment and achievement were measured. A value added score of 100 was considered to be satisfactory by OFSTED in that children had made the expected level of progress between KS1 and KS2. A further measurement of CVA added contextual information to the single value added score. Implications of this were considered by heads.

Good attainment at L4+ at the end of Key Stage 2 didn't necessarily give a good score for progress, which was dependent on the value added from Key

Stage 1-2. A school which would have done well in past inspections based purely on standards of attainment might subsequently be considered to be 'coasting' or performing inadequately. Conversely, a poor attainment score could still result in being judged as 'good' or 'outstanding' by OFSTED, if the school could demonstrate that they had made good progress from the baseline of Key Stage 1 and on entry to school in Reception. Satisfactory CVA seldom led to an 'outstanding' inspection, but satisfactory or even low attainment was still compatible with good CVA and, therefore, a 'good' inspection.

Heads felt they needed to understand the implications of the VA system on their intake:

> For example, if you have Chinese children, they count heavily against you and then as you go down the list you get to the zero effect, which is something like a non-FSM [Free School Meals], non-SEN [Special Educational Needs] white boy, or something like that, which has a zero effect on the results. As you look down the other end, it is a real hit-and-miss as to whether your school happens to contain people on free school meals, what background they are from . . . So if you have boys from Pakistan, free school meals and school action plus, you are well on the way! They are going to count really positively in your CVA. (Ht 18)

The majority of heads commented on CVA and were mixed in their evaluation of it. Mostly, their judgement depended on context. Those who benefited from CVA were more likely to advocate it:

> I think it is a much fairer system for schools like ours, which have real difficulties struggling with the attainment-only system. (Ht 15)
>
> Most of the schools it seems to me which are outstanding are inner city schools with over 101 CVA. The way it is calculated helps them. (Ht 17)

However, some heads disliked it for its inaccuracies, irrespective of their context:

> I think it [CVA] is blinkered, to be honest. (Ht 21)

For VA and CVA to be an effective measure of a child's and its school's performance, there has to be an accurate method of calculating and interpreting it. The added pressure for heads was that it was an inaccurate measurement and based on criteria such as FSM, which wasn't robust, as it relied on both accurate reporting of statistics by schools and for parents to apply for it, which it was perceived they sometimes didn't. Echoing Gorard (2006), heads cast doubt as to the accuracy of CVA data:

> I don't think it [CVA] is accurate enough but I think it never could be really because there are so many variables in it. (Ht 19)
>
> No, it's not accurate. Definitely not! (Ht 18)

The data collected for judgements was also considered to be inaccurate because of the quality of the SATs markers:

> The marking was done appallingly and we sent them [English papers] all back and they just wouldn't entertain them, but if you looked, every child was given the same marks for the first section, and that is ridiculous. (Ht 8)

The importance of the quality of inspectors was highlighted as an issue. There was a mixed response regarding the effectiveness of individuals:

> I think for me there is a recent frustration in that I can understand and interpret the data for my school . . . but when you have people who are coming to inspect your school and who can't really understand what you are putting in front of them, then I find it very frustrating. (Ht 15)

There was a more positive view of the quality of the judgements when they were made by HMI. One head made the point, 'Thank God it was HMI' (Ht 8), because her latest results had set her up for difficulties and she hoped he would look beyond the figures. Another experienced system leader commented:

> My dealing with HMI over the years has been much better than with OFSTED. I've seen OFSTED make silly decisions because they've let some schools off the hook and been unfair to others. (Ht 19)

Another aspect which impacted on the fairness of using data to judge progress was the opportunity for schools to manipulate it. The stakes were high because 'if the results are too high in KS1, then God help you!' (Ht 9):

> We are crap for value added because our KS1 results historically have been too good . . . we always pushed in year 2 to get good results for the children to get the best they possibly can, and what's wrong with that? (Ht 7)

Some heads believed they were hostages to fortune as they were not in control of the KS1 results. The view of this head of a junior school supports the general view that it was difficult for heads with just KS2 to prove progress:

> We are basically high achieving but we are a separate infant and junior school and so, of course, we have to very carefully watch the value added coming up from KS1 to KS2. (Ht 10)

The point widely made, however, was that it isn't that the KS1 tests weren't accurate in the past because of cheating or manipulation, just that the 'goal posts were different' (Ht 11). A child was awarded a level 3 even though it was just on the cusp of that level or a 3C. Heads, therefore, needed to ensure the child was 'securely Level 3B across the board' (Ht 12) in order for them to show the value added in Year 6:

> Five years ago, I would say go for it if there is a chance they can get a 3 but now it's around performance management and totality of performance. Is that child a 2B in your test and classroom assessment? Does a work sample reflect that? If so, then they are a 2B. (Ht 7)

The requirement to prove progress by the end of KS1 and KS2 meant a renewed emphasis on the accuracy of judgements determining baseline on entry to school:

> I feel I have got a more secure baseline to go from now and so that has helped people make better judgements . . . and, of course, it has been really important to do this to secure standards and progress. (Ht 18)

The importance of understanding the system and being able to argue their data and decisions to the advantage of the school is a key skill for heads. The majority of them expressed concern about the impact of their key stage results on their inspection. Nevertheless, as experienced heads, they could argue their data and decisions:

> I think I understood their agenda. What had happened was that as soon as I realised what CVA was going to do I had worked it out and sorted it . . . It's knowing what to say and how to contextualise. (Ht 3)

Heads commented that CVA was introduced because the government needed to find ways of encouraging practitioners to apply for challenging contexts. It was believed that aspiring heads would be otherwise reluctant to apply to schools where attainment was difficult to achieve. Even experienced heads commented that the public nature of the league tables was a pressure for those with below-average baselines of attainment for children on entry. This was despite the problem of accountability for heads in challenging circumstances being alleviated to some extent by the CVA system:

> In the end, though, the league tables don't help – its all about the comparison, and there is always somebody who is better, but, of course, half the schools are always going to be in the bottom half of the table no matter how good we all get, and its so depressing and demoralising for staff. (Ht 13)

It was widely anticipated that the Coalition government wouldn't keep the CVA judgement but that inspections would be heavily focused on standards and progress:

> CVA will go, but I think progress will remain. The two levels progress adjusted to your attainment will go. (Ht 27)

> I think they will still maintain that achievement is attainment and progress driven. I have had the experience at F and we had to prove to HMI that we had enough progress because standards were still a 4. (Ht 13)

Schools' self evaluation

The *New Relationship with Schools* (DfES/OFSTED, 2004) introduced the Section 5 framework, which was followed by the self-evaluation form (SEF) from 2005. While not statutory, there was an expectation by OFSTED that schools would complete a SEF, submitted online, which would be used to inform judgements made about the school.

Headteachers were aware of the importance of the SEF and used it strategically to show their schools how they wish them to be seen. An example of this 'fabrication' (Ball, 2001) was the need to present the school's data and the system of gathering it in order to present a coherent picture to inspectors:

> Our VA wasn't 100 when we were inspected and we got questions but what is important is the way in which you present the information to them. I presented the information to the inspectors in a way which enabled me to show good progress across the school. (Ht 12)

Heads used the SEF to manage the 'impression' they created (Webb, 2006) for inspection but resented the work intensification caused by the bureaucracy of its organization and structure:

> I resent the fact that the ECM agenda has led the way the SEF is organized, which I think is a 'rubbish' document in terms of the way it is structured. You could say it all so much more easily and to be forced to organize it in this way, well – it's just badly structured and I resent it. (Ht 14)

A small minority were more positive enjoying the structure and security it brought with it:

> I think the SEF is an important document. I have spent hours on it and I am on my fourth version of it . . . It keeps me focused on what I have got to do and I keep going back to it. (Ht 7)
>
> The SEF is a good way of summing up what the schools look like. (Ht 25)

When judging the leadership of the headteacher, it was important that the quality of teaching judgements made by the inspectors agreed with those of the school. Heads were encouraged to take up the offer of inspectors, if made, to jointly observe with them as a validation of judgements made in the SEF:

> I observed a lesson with the HMI and the first thing he said was, 'Well, what did you think? What feedback would you give that teacher?'. . . So it was reassuring that I picked the same strengths and weaknesses as he did. (Ht 11)

Time and familiarity with the SEF and the way the inspection schedule would be judged enabled heads to plan accordingly. The whole process was so formulaic, heads had resorted to referring to the number of 1 and 2 judgements they needed to illustrate with evidence in various sections in the SEF to be judged overall outstanding:

> We are at national standards at [base school]. In 2009, we had a fantastic cohort and in 2010 it was teacher assessed. We have got progress, though. You have to have enough 1s to balance it out. We would be a minimum of a 2 for capacity. (Ht 13)

It was announced by the then-Secretary of State Michael Gove in September 2010 that the requirement to complete a SEF was to be removed (National

Association of Headteachers [NAHT], 2010), but not the need to self evaluate. However, it was recognized that schools would still need a self-evaluation system:

> Actually, my SEFs were used on OFSTED training as to what they should look like and now they are taking them away! I will use them anyway as we have to show self evaluation. (Ht 25)

School Improvement Partners and Local Authorities

The 'single conversation' with a SIP was meant to reduce the impact of inspection on schools (Hopkins, 2005, 2006). They acted as an interim assessment, linking with schools self assessment. There were mixed reactions from heads regarding both the intention and outcomes of their conversations with SIPs during the research. At the beginning of the cycle there was a mixture of optimism, lack of understanding of the role and concern that the LA would lose knowledge of its schools:

> I think one of the positives is that they will be quality assured. They are hoping to bring in a national system of quality assurance so that every local authority in the country will have a good level of SIP. (Ht 10)

> I know we all criticise the LA and some of the advisers, but at least there was some level of continuity in that they could identify that there would be a problem at a particular school coming up. How is a school improvement partner going to do that? (Ht 16)

Heads were concerned about the definition of the SIP's role in terms of 'partner' or 'assessor'. One head, having trained as a SIP, had no doubts as to the relationship being definitely more along the lines of inspection. He commented on his training:

> It was a model for challenge, no support whatsoever and they didn't want to talk about support. Everything is down to standards, standards and more standards. So, I think SIPs are a bit of an issue. (Ht 5)

Many LAs trained their own advisers as SIPs, but this was identified as leading to a conflict of role:

> If I want to have a private and confidential conversation with my school improvement adviser about an issue I have got in school, then he is bound to be influenced

by what I have said when he comes in with his SIP hat on! It has to affect his judgement doesn't it? I mean it's not rocket science, is it! (Ht 18)

A SIP allocated to each of their schools caused an increased workload for system leaders. To alleviate this, headteachers Ht 13, Ht 20, Ht 25 ensured they had SIPs 'working across schools' (20). Some heads, such as headteachers Ht 15, Ht 22, and Ht 24 were SIPs and believed that they supported other heads when undertaking this role. However they questioned the expertise of those SIPs who hadn't led schools advising outstanding heads. Other views were that SIPs who were also LA advisers just compounded the ineffectiveness of LA provision and that the government would assume a lack of rigour in the process or collusion with heads.

The Coalition government announced the abolition of the SIP role as part of their aim to reduce bureaucracy (DfE, 2010b). There was general agreement that the partnership was not leading to school improvement and change was needed.

I don't think the government is happy that a lot of LAs have employed their own staff as SIPs. (Ht 23)

I think what they ended up doing through no fault of their own was being a bureaucrat or an administrator for the LA. What they didn't end up doing was leading identification and improvement in the school they were supporting. (Ht 27)

All they do is read the data and then you spend a whole day locked away writing their report with them three times a year and what does it do? Nothing! (Ht 19)

As a result of the white paper (DfE, 2010b), LAs will still have a monitoring role regarding the performance of schools. Heads commented that without capacity, how will LAs know there is failure in their local schools? However many also argued that as they were currently largely unsuccessful at monitoring or school improvement, it wouldn't make much difference:

[H]ow can schools like B and C exist when they have been monitored by the LA where you have a SIP going into the school a minimum of three times a year for the last three to four years, so how can writing of such poor quality be allowed to happen in Year 6? (Ht 11)

LAs make a judgement and say we won't send the Rottweiler in but then someone should give the . . . head a kick up the backside if it isn't working in that school and the LAs just won't come out and do it or are strong enough. I don't think the LA has the balls to do it, but I think the DfE has. (Ht 22)

Stress and inspection

The degree of stress in preparing for an inspection was varied. Some heads weren't worried because they perceived OFSTED to be formulaic and, therefore, easier to prepare for and because of their own experience:

> OFSTED is reassuring and I suppose having done it a few times I feel better about it. (Ht 15)

Heads that had recently improved the performance of their own or client schools, sometimes out of a failing category, were confident that OFSTED would validate the improvements made. These heads still had a degree of concern about proving their position but there was less of a direct pressure on them as they had experience of managing the process of inspection and tangible results which they could prove to OFSTED. Schools are monitored regularly in this position and so there is a strong element of the known situation for these heads due to the interim HMI monitoring reports. Ht 16 commented that HMI had said to her, 'We get you out of special measures.'

Heads were stressed to varying degrees, depending on their personal management of stress, about losing their high OFSTED ratings. Professional pride was important. Most heads might have felt a 'buzz' out of performing in difficult circumstances, but they were pressured to perform nevertheless, and it didn't diminish the focussed and relentless pressure they imposed on the school:

> Even before OFSTED, I knew that there was a danger of [supported school] going into a category because of the floor targets and I had to work hard to demonstrate that we know how we are going to get there. (Ht 24)
>
> I suppose it's keeping the momentum going after an 'outstanding' OFSTED. . . is the big one [issue] for me. (Ht 8)

For some heads, the results currently being attained by the pupils in their school gave them some level of security, providing they believed they could be maintained. This may have been due to high standards of attainment or the mitigation of good CVA.

One complicating factor, however, was timing. Heads identified the importance of the inspection to be timed in favour of the school's results, because if the inspectors came at the wrong time, there were fears low results would impact unfavourably on their inspection:

Three years ago, we had 12 children come from Jamaica in Year 6 and I would say
that eight of them had never been to school. It was terrible because they had to
be included in the results . . . It was a real, real bad year. (Ht 9)

Inspection was a stressful experience for almost all the heads, but particularly if
judged to be unfair. Examples of this are when a head believed that often 'OFSTED
responds to government papers or the agenda that's on offer' (Ht 17). Or:

If your argument is reasonable and you have got the evidence to prove it, then I will
debate with you all day long. But if inspectors are just going to sit and say, 'This is
what I think and you can do nothing about it' – then it worries me. (Ht 23)

Headteachers noted with varying degrees of anger and frustration that they
were in a vulnerable position due to the public nature of accountability. One
head linked her public accountability unfavourably to that of a GP, stating, 'I
couldn't pull off a report that says whether my GP is a good GP or not' (Ht 12).

Executive heads were accountable for their substantive schools and also for
the client school, which was either in special measures or vulnerable to failure. They commented on the impact failure would have on their reputation:

Well, I think you do feel occasionally, you have reached a height that some people
would love to see you fall, not that anyone has said it to my face. But, of course,
it would be wonderful gossip for at least a week. (Ht 19)

It worried me; in fact, it was the main thing which worried me about taking on the
role of National Leader of Education about how much would I be to blame about
a school being in difficulties. (Ht 17)

In 2010, the pressure of inspection for outstanding schools was removed, as
they would no longer be automatically inspected. HMCI also sent letters to
heads (Ht 23, Ht 25) informing them that the inspection for one or more of
their schools had been deferred until the next academic year due to satisfactory interim assessments of their performance:

Two of them [schools] got the 'golden ticket' from OFSTED to say they weren't
going to be inspected this year. That took a bit of the pressure off. (Ht 23)

Ironically, however, heads also noted that without inspection, it would be
harder to prove success. System leaders needed inspection because success would validate the leadership of the client schools when their current

reputation was based on success in the base school. When client schools have a successful inspection, there are a lot of 'kudos' (Ht 13) to be gained for system leaders because of an enhancement of their reputation.

New roles and new accountabilities

OFSTED and structural reform

The inspection system was unable to differentiate according to the needs of system leadership. The impact of multiple inspections for one federation was that the totality of performance for that federation couldn't be recognized, causing frustration:

> The team didn't understand the leadership role across the two schools. (Ht 19)

> So, if you are going to inspect five schools and four are working really well but one is trying to improve, what are you going to say that federation leadership and management is no good? How can that be when it is all right in those four schools? It must be judged on the federation's capacity to make a difference. (Ht 23)

In addition to a lack of understanding is a prejudice about the models:

> The one who inspected here just said, well, 'federation is like colonialism'. He said, 'As the headteacher of . . . school'. I said I am not the headteacher of this school. He said, 'I am inspecting this school and you are the head of it!' (Ht 23)

> When [supported school] was inspected in 2009 to come out of a category, the team I had was having none of the federation. I knew I had a battle on as soon as he walked in the door. (Ht 24)

Full schedule inspections across groups of schools were not part of the procedure at the beginning of 2011. The most OFSTED were able to offer was a 'leadership visit' (Ht 13):

> We had a federation OFSTED four or five weeks ago and got 'good' for leadership and management overall, [but] they were only looking at federation leadership in so far as sustaining improvement and driving ambition. (Ht 24)

OFSTED faced operational difficulties regarding the simultaneous inspection of schools. One reason was because of the timing of the inspections, with many schools in the middle of a cycle when collaboration was initiated, and so not due to be inspected. In addition, inspecting all schools at the same time might reduce some of the administrative burden and the stress of waiting for inspection. However, the practicalities were acknowledged as being difficult:

> It would be difficult for the head because you would be running between schools . . . It is hard enough anyway when they come because they just ask you for something at any moment . . . Sod's law would say you would be in the other school. (Ht 13)

> The only thing I am concerned about now is inspection. If they want to do both sites simultaneously that would be really hard work, as I would be darting between the two. (Ht 25)

While almost all heads felt there was no strategy for combining inspections, one head thought he had evidence of some strategic intention by OFSTED. All the schools in the forthcoming federation were inspected in 2009:

> Two out of the four schools were being inspected and the other two were due an inspection further down the line. 'A' was inspected six to nine months earlier than expected. So there must have been some strategic thinking going on somewhere. (Ht 26)

However, there is no other evidence from other heads to support this as a generalization.

The creation of a different form of academy by the Coalition government altered the relationship of these schools with OFSTED:

> They don't have any role to play in academies, but we are expecting them to pop in and see us because we are one of the first converters. (Ht 22)

In the previous two rounds, OFSTED would never have been referred to as 'popping in'. However, this didn't mean that this head, or other outstanding heads whose schools were unlikely to be inspected, agreed with the development:

> They aren't supposed to be inspecting outstanding schools, either. How ridiculous! You have only got to have a change of head or a slippage. We have gone over to another school and this one hasn't slipped but I could have turned my back on it and it could have slipped. (Ht 13)

> I am not sure how all these academies will be held to account by the DfE. Perhaps the DfE will have to grow enormously. OFSTED will be every couple of years but much lighter touch, maybe. (Ht 11)

Heads weren't complacent over their school's performance. Most of them bought in consultancy, they trusted in the form of external audit or used their own network of schools:

> Yes, but because we don't want to rest on our laurels we are going to appoint an HMI to do an inspection . . . [and] I want to get together with other outstanding academy heads and to inspect each others like an SIP. (Ht 22)

> All four of us go in like an inspection. We would deep slice the school and each of us have an area which we would go into and, unlike OFSTED, I would audit the business side of things as well such as the CRB checks or the contracts. I would do that every year. (Ht 23)

OFSTED: Children's Centres

The introduction of Children's Centres attached to schools meant changes to headteachers' roles within schools, due to the impact of governance and inspection. Heads were often unsure about the impact of accountability on their role if governors of the school were simultaneously governors of the Children's Centre, as described by this head:

> What exactly are you accountable for? . . . You are going to be a bit unsure about which part you are accountable for and which part the PCT [Primary Care Trust] people are accountable for. (Ht 5)

> I am worried about OFSTED with the Children's Centre. I am really quite concerned and I asked Christine Gilbert [Her Majesty's Chief Inspector(HMCI)] about that . . . and she said that she was sure that inspectors would be sensitive to the fact that Children's Centres were just developing, but I am not sure about that. I think they look at provision now, and I don't think they give two hoots about it developing. (Ht 13)

Heads were sometimes on the steering group of the Children's Centre when the centre was governed by the school's governing body, although this did not mean they felt they had any responsibility to line manage staff:

> From a building and site management side of things, the site manager is responsible. Because I am overseeing the site manager in school, then that is part of my remit . . . It is all one building and so we are responsible for it, but they are not my staff who are actually working in the Children's Centre part, and they are not accountable to me. So it is a grey area, isn't it? (Ht 8)

Other heads expected to be responsible for overseeing the running of the centre, either because they wanted the responsibility or felt they had no choice and were being pragmatic:

> I knew I would have to run it, anyway. In other words, it would be on my desk anyway, so I might as well run it through governors. (Ht 4)

The overall accountability led to increased workload and frustration for some:

> I have times when I think, please just take it away. I have been left with temporary contracts and it is a mess. I am not sure we see the outcomes for preschool children in the area. What difference is it making? (Ht 13)

It is by no means clear as to how the situation will develop. None of the heads had been inspected with the child care as part of the remit of the inspectors. I suspect that when they are, the expectations of OFSTED will steer them in the direction of their responsibilities.

Speculating on the future of accountability

At the end of 2010, there could only be informed speculation over the future of the inspection framework. Nevertheless, heads were keen to hypothesize on the future of accountability for schools:

> There will be that side of OFSTED which will keep an eye on academies but the role of the LA will be to sort out the schools where the data is showing they are failing . . . They don't have the personnel to deal with that, so they will have to commission that themselves. So they will look to commission school-to-school support but out of the schools which are successful. (Ht 23)
>
> I think the identification of schools in difficulty will be an initial desktop analysis of the school's data . . . If that throws up issues in more than one year, with say questions asked in the first year, then there will be some action taken. I think the department will develop a big team of advisers and I suspect the first action will be an adviser who will come into the school and ask some questions. My guess is that OFSTED will follow . . . Then the network of support will be put in with NLE or LLE support. (Ht 27)

There was some variability over the extent to which heads thought the system would be able to manage with an emasculated LA. Some thought that other schools and networks could easily pick it up, but others doubted there would be enough capacity in the system:

> It can't be outstanding schools, because there aren't enough of them. Even with 10 per cent of schools outstanding, and I don't think it's that high, they can't pick up all the others. So if the 'goods' are around 33 per cent of schools, some of those heads either won't want to help or are just not able to for some reason. I don't know how the monitoring role will happen without the LA. If they have a role – that has to be one. (Ht 13)

The idea of school-to-school support gained backing from heads but it was highlighted that peer support which has been commissioned due to failure isn't the same as:

> heads monitoring as peers . . . that is a very different system. It is one thing to go and support a weak school in crisis as a strong school but another to lead a cluster of good heads. I think they need to think that out very carefully. (Ht 13)

Would heads seek the role of cluster leadership? The reaction of Ht 22, who wished to lead up to 10 local schools, and others who are actively seeking to increase the size of their federations and to become teaching schools suggests that they would (see Chapter 5).

New roles accountability and earned autonomy

Their OFSTED rating meant that these heads could justifiably be considered to be in the category of having the 'required knowledge and skills' to be granted some form of earned autonomy (Barber, 2005) which was recognized:

> We are being pushed down the route of earning autonomy and the government is pushing the subliminal message that if you are doing a reasonable job, we are going to leave you alone. (Ht 18)

Elkins and Elliott (2004) argue that a degree of successful external accountability facilitated an independence within the framework of school leadership.

Heads recognized a degree of autonomy earned through a good inspection result but that this could change:

> Yes, it [success] does give you independence. (Ht 19)
>
> I think there is autonomy, but within very well-defined parameters of account-ability, and you had better not step outside those or you will be in all sorts of trouble. (Ht 5)

Not all heads had much 'faith in the reasons behind' heads being granted earned autonomy:

> It isn't really about being professional in your job; you only get autonomy if you are achieving the results in the tests. (Ht 7)
>
> I don't think heads are all that autonomous . . . In terms of the national agenda, then I think many heads allow the external agenda to dictate what they do and don't use it to work best for their schools. (Ht 3)

Success gives heads the independence which is absolutely crucial in a period of rapid change.

> Oh yes, I couldn't do what I do if people I worked with were interfering . . . I was talking to someone who was doing a strategy survey inspection . . . He said that everywhere he went, people in schools were gridlocked into systems they had to use but were going nowhere . . . and people in these schools had no opportunity to do what they think is best. (Ht 19)

Personality and inclination are important factors as heads shape their schools. Autonomy of action was assumed by them, as they were aware of becoming almost indispensable to the LAs to manage failing situations in schools. This degree of assumed power is evident in the comments of this head:

> To be honest, I have always done what I thought was right and in the best inter-ests of the school. I have always worked like that . . . and if they [inspectors] all want to argue it when they come, that's up to them. (Ht 21)

However, there are problems of isolation in being left alone:

> I think you can end up with more autonomy these days. But I think you also have the responsibility that goes with that, so it's a double-edged sword, really. It is a

very powerful job with autonomy, I suppose, but you can't hide behind anything. The buck stops with you and you are out there on your own. (Ht 18)

Ultimately, heads may be isolated figures, but in terms of managing their roles and leading strategically, they rely heavily on others, particularly staff.

The Strategic Leader: Building Capacity

7

Chapter Outline

Leading schools strategically as a mechanism for managing work intensification and empowering others is linked to leading successfully (Price Waterhouse Coopers, 2007). This chapter considers how workforce reform, distributed leadership and leadership development have been used as tools by headteachers to contend with the issues they encountered in leading change strategically to ensure sustainable leadership in single institutions, collaborations and federations.

Workforce reform

Remodelling the workforce

Performance management as a form of appraisal together with the obligation to give time for teachers for planning preparation and assessment were important aspects of workforce reform first introduced by the government in 2003. From September 2005 there was a requirement to remodel the workforce.

Although it had become a distant memory by the end of the interview cycle in 2011, its influence lingered on and allowed for the development of increasingly flexible staffing structures, which heads had used to build leadership capacity in the school.

Heads had different experiences and needs over why and how they should remodel, but most heads were, nevertheless, generally positive about the way they were able to use the process:

> TLRs [Teaching and Learning Responsibilities] were quite positive because it gave us the chance to rethink leadership and how we would want it to be restructured in a brave new world. (Ht 12)

When the need to remodel the staffing structure was introduced to schools in September 2005, it was not a new idea for them. However, the problem in managing the process was the disagreement between the policy-makers' TDA and Rewards and Incentives Group (RIG). By the time there was a model of guidance for the issue, it left very little time from September for the negotiation of the new structure and its agreement by December to take place. Therefore, the implementation of the procedure for remodelling caused considerable work and stress:

> I think the whole bureaucracy around it was ridiculous, really. All the work around the negotiations . . . (Ht17)
>
> You have to go to your governing body in September, then you have got to go back in December, then have it done for December 31, having gone back all the time . . . (Ht5)

The role of the LA was hardly mentioned in relation to the process of restructuring, except that, for two heads, it provided technical information around the personnel issues involved. Either the LA really had no part to play or it wasn't significant enough for heads to mention it, both of which are indicative of their diminished role in the organization of these schools.

There was some concern initially over the involvement of the unions and associations on the procedures to remodel the workforce. That they didn't speak with one accord was frustrating for the heads, as they weren't sure how to react with differing views and reactions from the unions and associations:

We are doing this [remodelling] with the NUT [National Union of Teachers] saying we are not playing, the NAHT saying we don't want to know about it. I had a stroppy letter from the GMB [General, Municipal, Boilermakers and Allied Trade Union] the other day – well, we haven't even got anybody in them! (Ht5)

There was potential for colleagues to be constrained in the process of remodelling through fear of confrontation with staff or unions:

I have spoken to people and they have gone for the very easy option and it's tempting because you think . . . oh gosh, the hassle that is involved, but then you have to think of the children and the school. It is an opportunity. (Ht 8)

Restructuring was quite a big issue in school . . . because we decided not to just keep the same. I know some people may have, but I think it is a mistake. (Ht 9)

There is some evidence later in the interviews that Ht 9 was right. Ht 7 in the revisit, two years after his initial comments about the possible difficulties encountered with union action, described how he eventually remodelled:

I ended up saying let's get on with life, really, and amending what I did because the first format I wouldn't have got through governors or staff. I would have had the NASUWT [[National Association of School Masters and Union of Women Teachers] crawling all over it as people would have lost out a lot. (Ht 7)

After a few years, the process of restructuring became an embedded practice to suit the changing staffing needs of their schools, as this head exemplified:

I suppose we restructured when we had to in 2005, but to keep the peace. Then, about two days later, I changed the structure, because once you had done it, you could undo it. You had to do it to a date, but then you could change as you liked. (Ht 19)

An important distinction is the extent to which heads used workforce reform as a tool to facilitate succession planning and new roles, or just to manage the perceived undoability of modern headship. The analysis is complicated in that it's sometimes difficult to distinguish their motives for decisions taken, because many of the heads were simultaneously undertaking workforce reform to enable them to lead as they wished in their substantive role with the increase in bureaucracy, as well as remodelling to build capacity for system leadership:

> No. Well, maybe partly about going out, but partly about leadership succession here. (Ht 17)
>
> Time management is always what you are up against as head of a school . . . I suppose it's one of the reasons why I developed the team the way I did. Not so I can go off and do other things. (Ht 18)

Remodelling and ECM

A factor in the decisions taken over staffing was the requirement to consider the needs of the ECM agenda when it was introduced into schools in 2005. This was in terms of new roles for heads with the imposition of Children's Centres on site and the extended schools agenda, as well as integrating the five outcomes into the curriculum, at the same time as remodelling the workforce. Many heads described how they had anticipated the agenda and recognized both ECM and remodelling as issues to be worked together:

> We've got three TLRs. One is for someone to look after the English and Maths and the standards for those, someone to look at the ECM agenda. (Ht 9)
>
> What I have tried to look at is someone for the extended curriculum, and someone for the ECM agenda . . . (Ht 8)

A third of the heads either had or thought they were going to have, and had planned for, a Children's Centre. All saw this as an opportunity for new roles to be created, as typified by these comments:

> I am hoping to appoint my Children's Centre manager from January. They wouldn't have anything to do because it's not even built yet but I will find them something to do. (Ht 4)
>
> We appointed to the Children's Centre in January [2007] and we have no building yet! (Ht 13)

Not only did a Children's Centre result in the employment of a manager, but also roles for others in school to manage the increased administration to cope with it, such as the appointment of a new office or business manager.

New and changing roles in staffing structures

Deputy and assistant headteachers and heads of school

There was an increase in the number and use of assistant headteachers and deputy headteachers appointed. The importance of the role of deputy and assistant heads in building capacity for new roles was recognized explicitly by most heads:

> I have had a really good deputy up to now who can manage in my absence . . . It's about capacity which changes of course. (Ht 3)

> I know when I am out, the place is being run extremely well, which is important. Mainly because I have got a brilliant deputy and she is superb. (Ht 5)

There was also the introduction of a new leadership role commonly referred to as 'head of school' and applied to the schools of Headteachers Ht 11, Ht 23, Ht 26, Ht 27. The role was in addition to the role of deputy heads and did not replace them. In these circumstances, executive headteachers had become removed from the traditional role of headteacher and appointed heads of school to undertake the day-to-day leadership in each school in a federation. However, even though heads of schools were undertaking some of the operational role of executive heads, the latter still saw their role as leading learning, just from a more detached position:

> I think my role is head of teaching and learning not a chief executive. I really believe that. I think that teaching and learning is the core business. (Ht 27)

Most heads of two school federations were prepared to distribute leadership but not to the extent that they devolved it entirely to a head of school:

> In terms of learning and teaching, the ex-deputy headteacher takes a lead in both schools . . . We don't have a head of school . . . accountable to a principal or director over both schools which I know that some federations do. I am very much, in real terms, the headteacher of both schools. (Ht 24)

The increase in the use of non-teaching support staff

Half of the headteachers in round one and two and all in round three identified an increase in the use of support staff, particularly administrative staff. This has increased overall staffing levels in schools over the last 6 years:

> Well, on the whole site, I have probably got 58 staff something like that now, and only 15 are teachers. (Ht 4)
>
> We have over 120 people who work here and that's grown in numbers and type of personnel. I know someone who used to be head of a very small nursery school and she said – 'Your job's like leading ICI!' (Ht 13)

For nearly a third of the headteachers in round 1 and 2 and all in round 3, the School Business Manager (SBM) or equivalent senior administrative person in small schools had become a key member of staff, often on the SLT. Frequently, business managers had responsibilities across schools:

> We have a school business manager and my bursar is working across all three schools. (Ht 11)
>
> My office manager works in both schools my professional assistant and HR manager work across both schools and so does the finance team. (Ht 20)
>
> I also have a very effective office manager and she has probably been more key to me being able to go out of school than anybody else. (Ht 17)

Headteacher Ht 23 has a business manager in each of the schools in the federation and, in addition, has appointed an overall federation business manager.

Building capacity within and across schools

Work intensification and headteachers

Heads became more experienced in building capacity in schools as system leadership grew as a role for them between 2006 and 2011. While their concerns about managing their extended role didn't decrease, their skills, knowledge and understanding in finding strategies to manage the situation did increase. The heads carefully considered the implications of undertaking new roles. While largely managing the roles and being open to doing them in the first place, heads nevertheless identified an intensification of work with new roles. They stressed the need to keep a balance of priorities which one of them referred to as 'keeping all the balls in the air' (Ht 3) and the work intensification caused by doing so. These examples illustrate this general feeling:

> I have to think how much capacity have I got to do this and not be dead at the end of it! If you constantly, every year, take on a new school with massive problems, think of how draining that is. (Ht 19)

> I had two days a week released here from my headship . . . to try and help set up the other school. So I was unpopular in my own school because I was away so much, and I was unpopular here, because I wasn't here the whole time. (Ht 11)

One way of managing work overload was to prioritize which roles to take up or leave, both in their school or other external roles, and choice was an important element in lessening the impact of work intensification:

> One of the reasons I gave up writing educational materials was that, while I absolutely love it and find it very rewarding, it wasn't bringing a huge amount into school in my role of headship. Something had to go and so that went. (Ht 12)

Employing teaching personnel was something most kept as part of their role, either as a single or executive head:

> I will know when we can take a risk with somebody or when we need a safe pair of hands. You get to know the right fit by how that person respects and responds to children that no tick list will ever give you. That's experience and that's your job as head. (Ht 23)

There were some heads in a variety of contexts that, despite the intensification of work, chose to take on significant roles themselves:

> My responsibilities are staff development and assessment coordinator but I have also recently picked up English and PSHE as well, and I do all the financial management in school as I have a particular interest in financial management. (Ht 22)

But this issue was complicated by the opportunity to distribute leadership for those leading small schools who were engaged in consultancy but not federation and so didn't gain from economies of scale.

> It's difficult because they talk about leadership giving lots of people responsibility, but when you are in a small school, there are only a few people you would give responsibility to, and so you have to do far more as a head. (Ht 9)

Credibility

Heads were aware of the importance of their credibility:

> The heads I am working with day to day want to work with someone who knows the day job and not someone sitting behind a desk at county hall and doesn't know the practice. I think that is crucial. (Ht 24)

> If leaders are going to support in schools, then they are going to observe lessons and what respect is there for someone who has never taught? The teachers would want to know what you are basing your judgement on if you have never been in front of a class. (Ht 25)

Changing relationships with staff

It depends on the individual headteacher as to whether they consult with staff before making the decision or inform them when it is a *fait accompli*. Nevertheless, there was a general recognition by heads that staff had a right to be part of the decision-making process.

It seems that a form of *permission* needs to be given by staff for heads to be able to play an extended role, because a lot of trust resides in the relationship. Heads considered this aspect of their role to ensure that everyone gained from the head's absence and staff weren't left 'feeling dumped' (Ht 12). Similarly:

> If you don't have relationships with your staff secure and in place and working well, you can forget doing anything else at all. (Ht 17)

The implications of a more strategic role for headteachers was 'letting go' (Ht 17). For some, this was difficult to come to terms with, particularly if they felt they would be more detached from children or the life of the school:

> You have to let go of it [school] and that is a very hard thing to do. (Ht 16)

> More of my conversations now are about the results and analysis and data and tracking than about the nitty-gritty of teaching and learning and the exciting part

about how you get children to learn . . . It's just the time . . . there is just so much else which has to be done. That's the worst. (Ht 14)

Relationships were reciprocal and heads reported that staff needed personal contact with them, too:

It's the things in school which can slip and people who should have been stroked haven't been because you haven't had time and somebody else has forgotten to stroke them in your absence. (Ht 3)

Staff are happy enough for me to go out to other schools, but I always have to touch base most days because they don't like not to see me. (Ht 17)

Relationships in client schools

Heads identified the need to establish relationships in the schools they supported. In some circumstances, there is a headteacher already present in the supported school joining a collaboration. This can cause some difficulty and is where the leadership of the system leader must be skilful in the management of relationships. For example, an NLE had been working with a head in special measures for some time, but after a third inadequate judgement by HMI, the LA had to act. It did so quickly and left the head with no option but to accept the NLE as executive head:

She was told on the Friday afternoon and I was in on the Monday morning . . . I was going to be executive head and that she would answer to me and I felt very insecure about that. (Ht 13)

Initially, staff in both base and client schools before federations were fully established were often unsure of the impact of the arrangements on their schools:

So, the good school says are they going to take us down with them or be a drain on our resources, will they be able to have our PTA funds? The school which has the most to gain is the most resistant because they feel it is a loss of their identity, loss of their school. Like a public failure. (Ht 23)

With a federation, there are two separate schools with different identities working together as one and that causes some difficulty initially, and there were bridges that needed building. (Ht 25)

Often, members of staff in the client school felt vulnerable to change, as identified by these heads:

> It was difficult initially from the point of view that the people at [the client] school were feeling worried and felt that here were people coming in to tell them what to do and I had to manage it fairly sensitively. (Ht 21)

> I am just seen as someone who is coming in to impose extra work. (Ht 26)

> We identified some very good staff but they had been told by the LA and everyone just to save the school and get the SATs results. But they didn't know how to do it, were inward looking and were just spiralling downwards. (Ht 24)

Visibility was more difficult for heads working on more than one site. Ht 26 highlighted how 'you are never in the right place'. Another:

> The most difficult thing in the first instance was time management, because you have got two sites several miles apart and so you have to decide how you are going to manage your time. (Ht 25)

Ht 23 had solved the problem of visibility in his federation by removing the expectation that he would be seen. It would be impossible to be on each site every day with a large federation.

Secondment

The strategies heads used to secure their schools depended on the extent to which they maintained involvement with them. A distinction must be drawn between those heads who were leaders across schools maintaining a role in their base school and those heads that were seconded full time to another school or other role, such as working abroad for a year (Ht 12) and working for a national agency (Ht 18).

Seven heads had undertaken a form of long-term secondment and believed the responsibility of leadership for staff to be far greater for those stepping up under such circumstances than for those leading alongside an executive head:

> It is different in some ways if you are going on a full time secondment. You then have to be prepared to let the person you leave behind to do the job. Even if they make decisions you disagree with, you have to let them do the job. (Ht 16)

Heads had to accept that, sometimes, the job would not be done in the way they would have hoped or that on return the school will have moved on:

> Before I went off on secondment in the autumn and spring term, everything was in place – the improvement plan the assessments were all in place, the SEF, everything was in place and ready. My argument was that the SLT just had to follow it! But it didn't quite work out like that and when I came back into school in the summer term this year – it was a nightmare! (Ht 18)

> Well, I had a secondment last year and so I am back in trying to get a pulse on everything that is happening in school, which is quite surprisingly difficult, having had a year out. (Ht 11)

Distributed leadership: consultancy, collaborations and federations

Heads entrusted their leadership and often reputation to the ability of staff to lead and manage in their absence:

> People have taken on more responsibility and they have said they feel trusted and have been given the chance to shine. (Ht 21)

Ensuring quality teams were in place able to step up into leadership roles together with changing existing structures were crucial elements in heads' decisions to undertake system leadership roles:

> I felt blessed with the leadership team at [base school] which were so skilled they were allowing me the time and freedom to pursue new work. I wasn't dealing with the mundane day to day as many colleagues were, and so I was thinking about where we were going. (Ht 24)

> You are taking key staff out of your base school and, of course, you are only there half the time and so it is looking at a completely different approach to leadership to what I had to do before. (Ht 19)

However, in delegating certain decisions to staff, heads had to accept that they may not make the ones that would be made by the heads themselves. It can cause heads concern, as this example illustrates:

> One or two times, I have felt seriously cross because when we decided to boycott the SATs a letter was sent out locally and we agreed not to meet with the parents.

> I found out that [SLT] held a meeting with parents. The parents were alright but what if they hadn't been? (Ht 13)

One head, when in the early stages of consultancy, felt she had neglected to ensure that staff were aware of the needs of the school from the onset:

> What I hadn't taken into consideration was that over the course of the year we have had a lot of new staff . . . I think we probably didn't put enough thought into inducting the more experienced teachers we appointed, and so I think a bit of the ethos in some of the ways I would want things done has slipped. (Ht 14)

The headteachers identified lines of communication and understanding of roles as important aspects of distributing leadership successfully in schools. These have often to be learned quickly, as circumstances can move fast when heads are called into other schools:

> Well, I think that if working in a role outside school is to work, there has to be a really clear definition and understanding of what the role of the next person in line is. (Ht 3)

> I think we need to think about what happens when heads are going to be in or out. If they are going to be out a day a week, then that needs negotiation with whoever is going to be head for that day and will they be paid for the acting headship for that day . . . If the head is out for the whole year, then what is the expectation of the people left behind? Are they just expected to mind the school or is development expected to take place? (Ht 12)

A consideration in the distribution of leadership and system leadership is over stretching capacity. This can occur either because the needs of the base school were underestimated:

> I drive all the assessment and I do all the analysis and it left a big gap. That was a mistake, really, because there wasn't anybody on the team who felt really comfortable doing that particular role. (Ht 18)

> Some people's response to being delegated responsibility is to turn into megalomaniacs and you don't always catch it for a long time if you are out. (Ht 16)

Or because the capacity of the system leader was stretched:

> I have to be in meetings all the time. OK some are partly self-imposed because I chose to do the CL (Consultant Leader) work, but . . . I am not even getting the time to walk around classes as you would normally do. (Ht 7)

> I would say I have probably taken my eye off the ball in this school. However, my focus has to be to support this other school because I feel so desperately sorry for the children there. (Ht 17)

Various models of distributed leadership were discussed in the base school:

> I have now got two deputies in this school and one which we call the national support school deputy who goes with me on other jobs. (Ht 19)
>
> I have had to restructure at the next tier down from me to ensure that all the day-to-day activities and routines and communication are working. (Ht 13)

And in client schools in collaborations or federations:

> Similarly, at [the client school] we have identified some staff who should have been management staff and are now leading areas in the school. The previous head kept everything in her basket. (Ht 24)

With established long-term school structures, heads began to talk about leading schools as a whole organization:

> Other people in both organizations report that they are absolutely confident when I am off site. It means that I can work in other schools or contribute to the NC or the DfE. All of this means that, in terms of system leadership, I have more time and capacity to impact on a whole range of different levels. (Ht 20)

Spreading good practice: working in other schools

All heads highlighted the overall benefits and the spread of good practice, which came with staff working across schools:

> For the first time, I got my team doing things and they went in and supported particular year groups on the quality of teaching and learning issues. They were supporting planning, working alongside staff and giving feedback, that kind of thing. I focused on trying to develop the middle leaders. (Ht 13)
>
> Well, if we could carry on with this school for the rest of the year, then the main advantage is that you would have massive capacity to improve because you have got a large staff which have had a lot of training and who are up for change. (Ht 19)

In addition, capacity was added to both supporting and supported schools:

> You start reading other people's improvement plans and philosophy and the vast majority of them give you a tour of the school and you come away thinking, oh, that's a good idea and you bring it back. (Ht 5)

The longer the collaboration had been in place, the more embedded became the practice of using staff across the whole organization. System leaders used the opportunity of deploying staff flexibly across schools to lead strategically and innovatively:

> I like to think differently and strategically, so if someone moves on in the federation, we don't just replace but think creatively about change or what is best. (Ht 24)

> We have got our curriculum coordinators sorted out across both schools . . . and now we have got a situation where we hold joint staff and governors meetings. (Ht 21)

> I think the idea of heads leading more than one school has enormous potential for securing schools, because I am able to keep people here by letting them do work over there. (Ht 20)

Staff could move permanently between organizations. One example was where staff applied for substantive posts in a federation where there weren't federation contracts:

> Three people have been appointed from [base school] to [client school], not seconded, but appointed. They have applied through the normal procedures and been appointed in more senior positions. (Ht 13)

Harris et al. (2006) note in their study that the executive head used the staff in the client school as part of the process for improvement, even if it altered the pace of working. This was recognized by heads in this study who wished to ensure continuity and entitlement. It manifested itself in terms of both training and innovation, irrespective of context, but there was some difference in the degree of success:

> We were able to include them on the performance training day that we had, so their leadership team got the training that our leadership teams did . . . but it's only going so far and it's frustrating. I mean we were going to have a leadership

> team meeting . . . But we organized it and when we got there, someone wasn't there and had forgotten, and that's frustrating. (Ht 14)

> I run the two schools a bit like a split site might be. So, innovations at the two schools tend to be paralleled, but the school which is the weaker school gets a simpler version of it. (Ht 19)

As organizations matured and practice became embedded, there was more opportunity to think long term. The disadvantages of impermanence of organizations when heads are seeking to lead strategically and innovatively were highlighted:

> The current impermanence has held me back. I have had to set up a temporary structure . . . However, what I haven't been able to do is to put a day-to-day head into the other school, or indeed here, and so I still have to do both. (Ht 13)

Can systems be replicated?

An issue in failing schools was dysfunctional systems caused by ineffective leadership as typified by this head:

> It had three years of capital money unspent. Massive under-spends in both schools and, frankly, it was a bit of a mess. There were no pupil-tracking systems in place or assessments, and teachers didn't know where the children were and ICT [Information and Communication Technology]was a mess. (Ht 25)

Heads discussed the concept of continuity of certain systems across the schools:

> I brought in systems from my previous school which I knew worked, such as assessment for learning and half-termly expectations for the planning. (Ht 25)

> So, we have aligned the two assessment systems . . . I think that is a good example of how there are benefits of the federation. (Ht 13)

However, transferring systems wasn't clear cut:

> It would depend on the school. If they were a school facing challenge in terms of outcomes, then maybe I would replicate the systems from [first school] . . . I think as far as systems and structures are concerned, some things would be easily transferable, but it would also depend on where it was. (Ht 24)

> I think what works here can't just be transferred and it doesn't work somewhere else. (Ht 22)

The need for internal consistencies between schools was highlighted by them in terms of both streamlining the leadership of a number of schools and ensuring the sustainability of improvement. This is particularly important for heads of several schools who need to be assured that if they are more strategic and less operationally involved, there is consistency in the group:

> What we have now is internal consistencies, which is 80 per cent of what all the schools must do . . . If you take the head of teaching and learning as running the school as their school, it is their school not mine, but they run it on an agreed system. (Ht 23)

> [We have] a single curriculum model and a single and simplified transfer and transition model. The curriculum is a better fit with agreed assessment regimes with the same information passed on. It is moderated so the benefits for the children have been great. Over time, I think we will see that more. (Ht 26)

> We have catering and premises managed across both schools. We are now moving the curriculum and policies. This is going to be like one large unified school. It is a new and different way of working. (Ht 19)

When asked what was the impact of the context of individual schools within a federation or collaboration, the consensus was that context and individuality could coexist with certain generic systems. These included staff deployment, tracking systems and rigorous assessment strategies, curriculum and teaching strategies to stimulate learning. However, there was also recognition that each school within the group still had a distinctive individual context, which Ht 23 referred to 'as the remaining 20 per cent'. What branding didn't mean was the loss of a cultural identity, as these comments illustrate:

> Yes, you can do it with policies and mission and values and behaviour policy. That is all shared. You can brand in that respect and share that definitely . . . but you can't brand something like Coca Cola does it. (Ht 25)

> I don't clone schools; they have their community and their context and they should be made great schools in that community and that context. What I do is I bring systems with me to help them develop in their own community and their own context. The systems I bring with me are not to turn a school into a clone of my other school. (Ht 27)

New roles job descriptions and contracts

Working at the edges of known practice meant that, to some extent, the heads had to adapt existing government policy and/or developing practices as they needed to. This often involved devising new job descriptions and contracts for their organizations. An example from this head describes the role of leaders of the federation:

> The leadership team is represented by me, who is the head of two middle schools, the head of the other middle school, and the head of the upper school . . .There isn't a job profile. It is something that we are making up as we go along. Just ensure that we hold each other to account and are mindful of what needs to be done and by whom. It is something that we decide between us. (Ht 26)

Another who issued federation contracts before they were official policy:

> In the last five to six years, practice has outstripped policy by miles and is accelerating away. An example of this is that we wanted federation contracts. It was never resolved, but we just went ahead and issued the contracts . . . and it is now a federation contract, which is policy by the back door. (Ht 23)

And again, a head who devised roles as experience dictated:

> I think the difficulty was however that because we were the first federation in . . . (LA) and because we wanted a different structure to what most federations perceive, like a head of school, people didn't understand the roles. The people who are now in the roles have developed them through and we had a vision of what the roles might be. But they have created them even more now, knowing what the federation needs. (Ht 24)

Many heads used federation contracts. However, they were not all the same:

> There is a federation contract with a school named in the contract, but it is made explicit that from time to time you may be asked either for a fixed-term or permanently to spend time in one of the four schools if needed. (Ht 26)

In another example, staff could either transfer to the federation contract or could elect to retain the school's original contract:

> Every year, they [staff] are offered the opportunity to change, but you cannot insist on people taking them up who are already working here – that is the legal side. Their contract is assigned. (Ht 23)

Ht 27 was proposing to set up federation contracts and:

> since last June I haven't appointed anyone without an agreement that they would
> be prepared to work in any other schools . . . In, let's say, my original school, I have
> about two-thirds who would be happy to work in any school and about one-third
> who are very established in the original school and would find that harder. I have
> no problem with that. What they know is that if they want to be considered for
> promotion, they have to be prepared to work in any one of the schools.

The situation for collaborations which had more than one governing body
was different from federations, as there was no guarantee the schools would
remain together. Nevertheless, there were still embedded working practices
regarding staff working across schools. In the example below, the contracts
were held by one school and worked charged to the other school/s:

> The job descriptions which are across both schools say that you will be working
> across both schools and what is expected of you. (Ht 20)

Ht 19 led a collaboration in round two but when revisited in round three
had moved to a school which then became federated. She described the
differences:

> Here there are federation contracts. In my old schools, we weren't a federation, as
> there were two governing bodies . . . Here, though, we have one governing body
> and it's becoming one entity, as much as possible. (Ht 19)

The decision for placing staff in one school or another depended 'on the logis-
tics and necessities of it' (Ht 26). The advantages were seen to accrue to staff
as well as the schools:

> If you take that you have an issue of a falling role in one school, then you have
> to make a redundancy, but in a federation, you have to move them to a vacancy
> elsewhere. They are moving within an organization they already work in and so it
> is much more secure. (Ht 23)

Headteachers' changing leadership practice

Lack of direct power to make changes can be one of the disadvantages of the
role as a consultant head. Evidence to support the importance of clarity of
role and autonomy from this consultant leader:

Our brief was to support in raising SATs results, but it's too short term. I would like to have the opportunity to do more focused work and stay for a couple of weeks and stay there and follow through, instead of revisiting conversations because you were coming back and forth. (Ht 9)

Leading long-term collaborations or federations requires a different form of leadership, which was widely recognized:

If you are a federated head, it is much more strategic. You might have a similar vision for the schools and overall educational aims, but you aren't the one driving to get there necessarily but are monitoring how others get there. (Ht 25)

I suppose that I am still doing some of the observations and keeping my hand in, but more and more, I am just getting impact reports over what is happening and monitoring from the different areas, and so what I am getting is an overview of what is happening. (Ht 8)

It was important for heads to establish their credibility and manage crises in failing schools, and this sometimes involved a more operational role, if only in the short term:

My difficulty was that it was me in there four days a week and nothing else . . . I was using skills I hadn't used since a deputy and the first couple of years as head because I was literally talking to parents about the toilets and head lice. I wasn't doing a visionary strategic role; I was just doing the day-to-day role. (Ht 24)

So much energy just goes into getting things done. You've got children misbehaving to sort and get an air of calmness into the school. In [client school] I have been kicked, spat at and sworn at more in the first few weeks there than I have been in 30 years elsewhere. (Ht 11)

Larger schools of two- and three-form entry had greater capacity to support, enabling heads to take staff to work across schools at short notice:

I was just picking up the phone every day and saying I needed somebody here or there . . . We had capacity at [base school] but not as much as I needed, which really put the pressure on them. (Ht 13)

In these circumstances, it isn't possible for heads to apply a strategic plan to working in other schools, as they are working in unknown circumstances and under pressure. However, while trying to achieve stability and quick wins, heads acknowledged that this shouldn't be at the expense of long-term 'sustainability and systemic change' (Ht 24).

Succession management and system leadership

Developing staff is important for ensuring the quality of learning for children and securing the sustainability of the organization through attracting and recruiting new high-quality staff and retaining and growing those in post:

> It isn't about the curriculum or class size or what is centrally enforced, but it is about the quality of teachers and it starts with who is selected. (Ht 14)

Having selected well, heads were keen to develop the leadership skill of staff and grow them into new roles. They acknowledged this as enabling school improvement and retaining staff:

> I have people who are quite ambitious and want to get on and see the federation work is giving them the experience they need to get on for promotion. (Ht 13)
>
> There is virtually no turnover of staff at all . . . and what people say to me is they will go and work in another school as part of their role but there is no way they get the kind of opportunities they get here . . . We have got some movement in the leadership team this year . . . but I have people from here stepping into their shoes. (Ht 20)

The opportunities staff would gain in a National Support School (NSS) were highlighted:

> I must admit that the NSS status seems to have brought us career staff . . . We really push that there are lots of leadership opportunities when we try to get staff. (Ht 19)
>
> I think it helps to keep staff here. It gives them the experience of being a head in my absence, without having to be a head. (Ht 14)
>
> Staff have not just been willing to do more but have actually sought to, because they have seen it is going to be good for them and so I think it will be good for the system, as well. (Ht 13)

The benefits of being an academy were also considered an advantage for recruitment for those heads of collaborations or federations considering academy status:

> I think the academy status is good for recruitment and a few weeks earlier we would have been struggling to get applicants. (Ht 11)

Many heads keep their staff and grow their own, but the system can benefit, too:

> People have left the school as a result of their success here and what they have done particularly after the first year of federation . . . the deputy is now an executive deputy . . . and being utilized across schools . . . So it isn't just about keeping people, it is also about giving them the skills and opportunities they can then use in another school or for promotion. (Ht 24)

Heads considered the capacity of the system to manage system leadership roles when this generation is due to retire:

> I suppose the worry is that over the next four to five years are the new heads coming up able to manage it. I think NPQH is good, but I have a slight worry that the practice is different from theory. (Ht 11)

> If you take four schools with up to 600 in them, it would be a big job for one federation head of them, and what happens when the experienced heads retire? What happens at the end of five years? (Ht 19)

A solution was for staff to step up:

> We should be considering training up our successor . . . and it's what we have planned and she is going to take over [base school], but I am suggesting to governors I think that she takes over as head of both schools. (Ht 21)

Heads acknowledged that the system needed to consider the training of successors to secure the future quality of school leadership:

> I also think there is still a lot to be done regarding leaders of the future. We still have a massive recruitment issue of getting the right leaders into our schools. (Ht 24)

Leadership development for headteachers

The intensified workload of headteachers meant they lacked time for CPD:

> When I became an NLE I became divorced from relationships and networks I had with other headteachers because of becoming so involved in working with other schools. You move away from regular CPD . . . I can see the benefit of some sought of network for NLEs. (Ht 14)

There was evidence that if conferences, seminars or training were considered good CPD, then heads would make the required effort to source it:

> I drove all the way up from here to Nottingham [National College] that morning on the back of the names of the people who were there . . . So, if I admire a person and their name crops up, I will come to it. (Ht 22)

And the scarcity of relevant training was highlighted:

> I've identified that there is a gap for the training of heads or aspiring heads of more than one school. (Ht 24)
>
> I don't think that NPQH would prepare someone for executive leadership. It has an emotional journey of its own. You are somewhere between a professional governor and the occasional visitor. (Ht 26)

Preparing a leadership development programme for those whose practice is often ahead of policy is a challenge:

> What they haven't done is try to establish what it means to be an executive head and what makes you tick. (Ht 23)
>
> It is difficult to put a training package together, as people are doing such different things. (Ht 19)

Suggestions were made by the headteachers for what might be required as part of such leadership development. These included developing a vision for what the federation could look like in different circumstances; governance of more than one school; developing leadership structures in schools especially at the beginning of system leadership when few systems exist; dealing with staffing issues such as sickness, poor capacity and incompetence; an understanding of what systems are needed in schools and the issues involved when transferring or implementing new systems:

> I think we need to think about teasing out what are those systems which we need such as job profiles, for example, which need to be clear. (Ht 26)

Ht 13 highlighted the differences in working in a weaker school for those who were inexperienced as system leaders:

> Going into a weak school, you have to be much more direct, challenging, tougher, time limited and it would have been good to have thought all this through first. (Ht 13)

There was speculation where the training for system leadership would come from apart from that offered by the National College, and Ht 26 highlighted the benefits of 'good commercial systems'.

One head didn't think she needed training as part of a programme, but thought it would be important to network with clusters to share school practice and particularly to:

> Talk to like-minded people and how to go out of this school and help people get to the emotional state that is ready to engage in the work that we do. (Ht 22)

Ht 26 offered a note of caution in relying on the views of other heads to make decisions and that their success may be due to the effects of personality rather than a tried system. He commented that such practice hadn't been 'systemized', and so may be unreliable.

The role of schools themselves in the development of training for senior leaders across schools as well as for initial teacher training was greeted with enthusiasm:

> What we are pursuing is for [base school] to become a training or teaching school. (Ht 11)

But, there was also a role for traditional leadership development, as this head noted:

> LPSH . . . was the first time I had done a 360 and thought about my own leadership. I hope that type of leadership development remains, as that is something for heads especially which the college has done and done well. (Ht 14)

Finally, one difficulty for providers is the credibility of those presenting or leading training for system leaders:

> The system is so fast moving that I can't rate anyone who hasn't been in schools and a lot of people don't know what it is like to run a school, and so I think, what's the point of them telling me to be honest. (Ht 22)

One other means of leadership development for system leaders is expensive but 'invaluable' for one head, who had experienced coaching as part of his leadership programme:

> To have someone at the end of the telephone and to be able to touch base regularly is really, really interesting and challenges the way you might lead and tackle instances. (Ht 26)

No one highlighted LAs as deliverers of training services for system leaders:

> If I have wanted to pursue something further, then I've used the National College or SSAT [Specialist Schools and Academies Trust] and I have used external agencies like that in order to help me with my strategic thinking. The LA would be the *last* place I would go! (Ht 22)
>
> I don't buy anything from the LA because I don't need to, and I don't intend to, and I can always get probably a better service elsewhere. (Ht 20)

Long-term effects of system leadership on schools: sustainability

Heads recognized the difficulties schools would have if system leaders left. First, it could be financial if the base school relies on the finance of the system leader to pay for other roles created in schools or other resources. Ht 8 identified finance being allocated to building a 'new classroom' and another as follows:

> It does worry me that if this school doesn't come out of special measures then I won't go to another school, which will have implications for the funding that I need to keep this school running how I want it to. (Ht 17)

Secondly, the head may have involved so many staff across schools it may be difficult to unravel the roles if it becomes necessary to do so if the federation breaks up for any reason. Thirdly, it was recognized that, sometimes, the success of system leadership rested on the system leader, but this was unsustainable:

> I think in the infancy of federations in this country it was the people with the charisma that could take the communities with them. They could stand at the front and convince the people that it was the thing to do. But that's only good enough to get things going . . . The system shouldn't depend on that. (Ht 23)

> You can get the charismatic leader that can take everyone with them, but take them out of that position and what have you got? All that flies in the face of using leadership teams and sharing leadership. The power of one is quite a dangerous place to be in if there isn't the system alongside it. (Ht 26)

A point made by a head about her own federation:

> The question is – is the federation me? I don't mean that arrogantly, but if I decide to go or retire, would they want to keep the federation going? Say if nobody applied internally, which could happen, would they bring in a federation head? (Ht 13)

One issue was the role of the LA in sustaining new models. Ht 24 believed the LA didn't always understand:

> They think about the here and now and not the changes in the system for the future. (Ht 24)

The need for adequate funding to sustain improvement was highlighted:

> To do that, we have to have the capacity, and that comes down to money, because, inevitably, schools have to be funded properly to have the capacity in their own schools to be able to use it in others. (Ht 14)

One issue regarding sustainability is the permanence of the collaboration or federation arrangements for the schools involved. Heads organized federations so that when they left the structure would be sustained:

> The whole focus is going to be about pooling their expertise and working with other schools. They won't be able to choose not to be part of it and we are trying to recruit and appoint on the basis that there is an ongoing collaboration. (Ht 11)

Formalizing collaborations was believed by heads to be more beneficial for sustainability and school improvement than a network or cluster of heads of different schools might be, as typified by this head:

> You only need one person to procrastinate, miss a meeting and it completely collapses. So while you might get the majority at the table it only takes one not to be there and it just doesn't work. There is lots of fine talk. (Ht 26)

But under a formalized arrangement:

> If someone says something is happening, then we can say, 'All right we will come and see it in action'. And we do. (Ht 26)

Part 3
Findings and Implications for School Leadership and Government Policy

Key Findings for School Leadership

8

Chapter Outline

Headteachers were aware of the educational agenda for change and taking advantage of the wide-ranging new roles being offered to or imposed on effective school leaders, which changed their roles significantly, with corresponding implications for their schools as an organization. The following key findings are a reflection of the consequences of the changing role of the headteacher as they react to government-imposed change:

1. The development of new internal and external roles for headteachers.
2. There were changes to the role of governors as a result of changes to the role of headteachers and school organizations.

3. New roles for headteachers led to new and changing relationships with Local Authorities and the National College.
4. There has been an increase in the strategic role of the headteacher with the development of new roles for staff.
5. Leadership styles have been adapted to manage new roles and build capacity in their school/s.
6. The effects of accountability have impacted strongly on the actions and reactions of headteachers.
7. There was evidence of earned autonomy and heads implementing government policy with a mixed picture of compliance, mediation and subversion.

A review of these key findings forms the basis of the rest of this chapter.

The development of new internal and external roles for headteachers

Headteachers' roles were wide ranging, with an increasing number of external partnerships, collaborations and membership of various clusters and networks. They identified the following reasons as to why new roles were being made available to them:

- Government's response to the undoability of traditional headship by providing ways of allowing heads to lead more strategically and manage workload.
- The introduction of new roles, such as executive headship, were judged to be a response, by stretching leadership, to the imminent retirement of the 'baby boomer' generation and lack of interest of suitable successors in headship.
- The impact of ECM in establishing new relationships and leadership and management practices.
- To raise standards and effectiveness in vulnerable schools through the process of collaboration.

While most heads identified the same reasons for change, they didn't all agree that the issues they identified for others were applicable to them. The timing of the interview was important in this finding. There was considerable concern over the undoability of the role and the amount of bureaucracy surrounding it in the first round of interviews. Most heads recognized intensification of work as an issue, but by the second round had found ways of managing it through distributed leadership and reforming the workforce so it wasn't undoable in their context.

There was considerable speculation by the heads as to how their role would change and differences in understanding as to how future headship would develop. Most heads recognized that the future would involve more school-to-school support. Towards the end of the interviews, some heads were identifying their involvement in the traditional role of LAs and the opportunity they had to offer their own school improvement packages across schools and localities.

Whatever their opinion as to the desirability of it, the headteachers were aware of messages that the school leader of the future didn't have to be head*teacher* (Price Waterhouse Coopers, 2007). There was some openness to this idea in the first two rounds. However, by the third round, heads were convinced that while the role of headteacher would change, school leaders would require the deep understanding of education that only those practitioners with QTS can bring.

Types of new roles

Categories of headship roles (*Fig. 8.1*)

Group 1 Buccaneers	Group 2 Gurus	Group 3 Pioneers	Group 4 Heretics
1, 2, 3, 4, 5, 7, 8, 9, 10, 11, 12, 13, 14, 15, 16, 17, 19, 20, 21, 22, 23, 24, 25, 26, 27	3, 4, 5, 7, 8, 9, 10, 11, 12, 13, 14, 15, 17, 18, 19, 22, 24, 27	2, 3, 4, 5, 8, 13, 15, 16, 19, 22, 24	6

Figure 8.1 The presence of heads' roles in more than one group reflects that they have more than one role.

Buccaneers 93 per cent of the heads were linked to roles involving system leadership with one or more schools to engage with them directly in school improvement. Heads were often working at the margins of what was policy because they took action (such as with the allocation of staffing across schools, and initiating federation contracts) that the system hadn't yet micro-managed. These leaders were CLs, NLEs and executive heads, and all were involved in working in one or more schools which had been deemed by LAs or OFSTED to be failing to provide an acceptable standard of education for children. In many circumstances, the federations continued and expanded after the failures in the supported school had been eradicated.

Gurus 67 per cent of the heads were system advisers. While these roles with agencies such as OFSTED, LA. SIP, DCSF/DfE, NC, QCA and British council were also external to the school, I have not defined the work as system leadership. While heads undertaking these roles were still involved in school improvement issues in education, they were more detached from it. They were not by definition directly involved in finding *solutions* for raising the level of provision in an individual school other than their own.

Pioneers 41 per cent of the heads had a new role but located within an individual school. This included leadership of a primary academy, co-located school or extended organization with a Children's Centre or who were co-leaders. In addition, there were several heads such as Headteachers 11, 23, 26 who were planning academy conversion for one or more schools. As this role was pending, they haven't been included in this statistic. However, I was made aware that subsequently their application for academy status for their schools was successful.

Heretics 0.04 per cent, or only one head from the first round, didn't have a new internal or substantial external role.

The categorizing of the heads' membership of these groups, while indicating the extent of their number engaged in a range and variety of the roles in the research, doesn't give an indication of the extent to which these roles were pursued. The range was from very little in one case to extensive and wide ranging for the majority of the sample. This complicates grouping because, sometimes, heads had experience of different roles simultaneously as well as moving in and out of roles.

External roles

System leadership is producing a new type of school leader and is more widespread and embedded due to the role of support schools than that of the single heroic superhead. System leadership is not necessarily another layer of hierarchy of school leadership but can be part of an emerging pattern of different models of leadership and a strand in the professional repertoire of some headteachers.

Consultant leadership, secondment and executive headship for example could be short or long term, depending on the needs of the school and availability of the headteacher, which changed according to inclination and demand. Although the extent of partnership changed, there was universal agreement that schools working together in partnerships are more than the sum of their parts as individual schools. Collaboration improves their own schools, those in the locality and, consequently, across the system. They maximize capacity in the locality and system and help to create sustainability by picking up failure in the group and raising aspirations.

An important consideration as the trend for school-to-school support grows is that, while the system leaders may be successful in turning schools around, this doesn't mean there is a always a corresponding likelihood of this improvement being sustained. Heads recognized the problem of system leaders being stretched too far and the implications of this for succession when they leave. Ensuring sustainability was usually part of an exit strategy for heads involved in these roles. In the third round, sustainability of improvement was secured by the supported schools becoming part of a long-term or permanent collaboration or federation. Many heads were already planning for their exit by identifying their successor from within their schools.

School Improvement Partner (SIP)

While SIPs were used, they had a significant role to play in the external role for some headteachers and on the workload of all. There were contrasting views regarding the value of SIPs in supporting and challenging headteachers and the extent to which they were assessors or partners. However, during the interviews, headteachers were increasingly describing the work of SIPs in ways which indicates that they were identifiers of problems in schools and that if they worked towards a solution then it was because of individual relationships made. Due to the power dynamic within the relationship of SIPs and heads, which is different to that of CLs, NLEs and LLEs, and the operation of a pre-determined agenda, SIPs are not in the same category as system leaders.

There was also an issue of quality assuring the effectiveness of SIPs who were identified as being of variable quality by heads. Ht 10 suggested this was government's intention but it didn't transpire as a national accountability procedure. Many SIPs were quality assured by the LAs they worked for but this was considered to be an unsatisfactory process lacking rigour and independence by heads and few mourned the loss of the role in 2010.

National Leaders of Education (NLEs)

The role of NLE was unknown in the first round of interviews but caused some interest in the second round. Some of the heads who weren't NLEs when interviewed subsequently became them afterwards, which I identified from re-interviewing or from the list on the college website.

This included headteachers 8, 9, 10, 13, 15. In the third round, while not a prerequisite for interview, I found that of the six new interviewees, three were NLEs at the time of interview and two more were granted the status afterwards.

The interest shown in the role of NLE is indicative of the success National College has had in promoting it. Heads identified the role in common with Chapman et al. (2008) as being part of the government's strategy to combat the 'educational failure' of some schools, but in addition also thought it was a measure introduced by the government as a way of 'getting around Local Authorities where Local Authorities are not effective' (Ht 20).

They were aware that the role was monitored by National College for impact on raising standards in supported schools and according to the maintenance of an 'outstanding' leadership rating by OFSTED for the NLE. They accepted this and, while concerned to acknowledge the 'privilege' of the role (Ht 26), nevertheless were aware of its status and the enhancement of their reputations in the wider local and national system. This brought NLEs opportunities to advise government ministers and working groups with the National College and DfE. All were involved in a variety of work, ranging from using their staff and themselves as consultants in other schools to a more long-term collaborative arrangement and permanent federations. The choice lay with the system leader and so they operated with a considerable degree of power and influence within the school system.

Executive headteachers

The role of executive head was a growing phenomenon during the time of the study and was a particular feature of the second and third rounds. While the federations were contextually different, a feature of all but one of them (Ht 26) was that they were created initially to support schools perceived as failing. Some of these federations grew to include schools for reasons other than failure, usually as a response to managing succession and the viability of small schools.

There may be a limit to the size of federations due to scale and geography which can be led by those heads who want to remain close to the role of lead learner. As the role involves a strong operational element, sometimes daily or part of each week, it was felt that the optimum size would be two schools or a maximum of three. Heads led larger federations but it was a different form of school leadership. While still strongly involved in the quality of learning they employed another tier of leadership, head of school, or similar to manage much of the traditional role of headship.

A sense of ownership and power was a key difference between the attitude of heads who were working as school leaders in long-term or permanent arrangements and those who were working on short-term collaborations or consultancy, especially if an existing head was in post. Federation heads all treated the supported school/s as extensions of their base school, with posts which were created specifically as a result of the federation such as a deputy head across both schools (Ht 19), or heads of schools (Ht 11, Ht 23, Ht 26, Ht 27) or for administrative support (Ht 20, Ht 23, Ht 25).

Heads recognized that roles across schools brought economies of scale and other benefits such as staffs' professional development. They speculated on the increase of chains of schools and the branding of systems within federations. They were prepared to use similar operational systems for alignment such as a common framework for assessment in their federations but reinforced that this was their choice. Citing a perceived lack of autonomy, they resisted the opportunity to be part of a chain of schools with a sponsor.

Internal roles and ECM

National College has promoted the importance of high-quality multi-agency relationships (Coleman, 2006, modified 2009) to ensure the successful leadership of extended schools. There was a mixed reaction to this and none of the heads anticipated high-quality relationships with other agencies. The main reason for their cynicism was not so much the extra work, which they had strategically managed successfully, but the unfairness of them having to sort out the problems caused by the inefficiency of others as they perceived it. Therefore, there was a high degree of both resentment and cynicism about the extended schools' agenda and their role within it from most of the heads but this was tempered by their willingness to work towards it for the benefit of the community.

The accountability for the leadership of Children's Centres was not largely understood. The key is governance. If the school's governing body was the main accountable body, then this was separate to their role as governors of the school (DfES, 2007). However, in practical terms, the existence of such a Children's Centre under the same governance as the school meant that the responsibility for the leadership of the organization cascaded to the headteacher as the school leader. The degree of direct accountability for this was unclear to the heads but was an issue for them as much of it was assumed and unformulated. They accepted accountability because if they were going to be responsible for the centre, they felt it was important to have overall control of its direction through the governing body.

Future roles: teaching schools and primary academies

Some heads were investigating the possibilities of becoming a teaching school, especially if they were NLEs or already had accredited school status. Other than speculating on the possibilities for their schools of further local influence, the role was too late to be included in the interview analysis. However, heads' interest is indicative of their political acumen and drive to stay ahead of the game and I learnt later that several had applied but decisions came too late to be included in these findings.

Early indications show that the decision to convert to an academy seems to be determined by the relationship heads had with their LAs, budgetary considerations and a wish to shape the future of their school/s. Most heads believed that these issues and the increasing number of schools converting will create a tipping point, at which all schools will be driven to convert. Only one head had converted to an academy during the interview period and three others had applications lodged with ministers, which were subsequently successful. One head intended to resist this perceived pressure for as long as she could. Other heads were cautious either because they felt the LA had little impact on their role and so leaving the LA wasn't a driver for change or because of a concern regarding the costs of being a standalone primary school if the initial increase in budget wasn't sustained.

Headteachers' motivation for new roles

Some heads were purposively seeking a wide menu of opportunities and for a variety of reasons, which supports the early findings of (Earley and Weindling, 2006). The financial reward for the heads was variable but could be considerable with 'entrapment of salary' (Ht 19) or the difficulty of being able to match a high salary elsewhere, being specifically mentioned.

However, financial reward wasn't the main motivation for any of them, despite the fact that there were wide discrepancies of pay. Most heads declared that their main motivation was professional growth and challenge, underpinned by moral purpose. Leaving to undertake other roles was not attractive to the heads. The reasons given were that it was more difficult to make a difference to children, the working practices and lack of autonomy in other roles.

The changing role of governors

The scope and variety of decisions governors have to make have increased considerably as new roles such as executive headship and NLE have become available for heads. This has through necessity changed the relationships between headteachers and governors, as heads have had to work with governors more closely and strategically over their changing role and the changing position of the school as an organization. The type of relationship heads had with the governing body depended to some extent on whether headteachers felt that governors understood the issues for which they were responsible and, in particular, the demands of the role of headship.

Governors had to agree to heads undertaking new roles in other schools or for schools to federate or become an academy. In some circumstances, such as long-term collaborations or federations, they became members of the governing body of other schools or part of a merger with the governing body of another school/s in a federation.

No head was ultimately unsuccessful in pursuing the roles they wanted but the degree of difficulty in obtaining them was variable. Generally, the compliance of governors in agreeing to new roles for headteachers was less because they understood or were interested in the benefits of system leadership to the wider system and more because they felt that not to comply might mean they would lose their headteacher. However, there were two exceptions (Ht 23, Ht 26) where governors were being proactive in the decision to federate or add more schools to the federation.

Governors and accountability

There was a benevolent attitude towards governors from most of the heads, in so far as the heads appreciated the support they received in undertaking their various duties and responsibilities. Nevertheless, there was some resentment over the position governors had been granted by the government in holding heads to account and with their changing role. The requirement by government to explain complicated policies and agendas to governors in different ways, and on several occasions was a source of frustration identified by most of the heads.

One exception to this general resentment was the strong relationship developed between heads and chairs of governors. The role of chair has been strengthened due to their strategic importance to headteachers as new school structures developed. There was evidence that, as governing bodies changed and became smaller and more strategic in academies or federations, they also became more professional. One head was involved with the chair in choosing governors for the academy and this invests an enormous power and responsibility in both.

Just to consider governors as blind in their support, or easily led, however could be unfair to those governors who were supporting their own headteachers. This judgement is based on the fact that the heads in the sample were very good to outstanding. The issue of trust and professional respect felt by the governors towards the headteachers had a bearing on the latter's opportunity to enjoy a degree of earned autonomy.

New and changing relationships with Local Authorities and National College

Changing relationships with LAs

The involvement of the LAs in school improvement and their relationships with heads in this study was variable. Nevertheless, evidence points to them becoming increasingly involved in the external roles of heads by brokering their support for school improvement and through their involvement with National College. They were acting as brokers for NLEs and LLEs as well as becoming more involved with the college in projects such as those involved with succession planning (Local Solutions) and the CPD of aspiring heads (NPQH). As the internal capacity of the LAs diminished, some heads were becoming part of the accountability system as they were used by LAs to take the place of advisers in reviewing schools and as SIPs.

In general, the relationships between the LAs and the heads they used for support were cordial. This depended on the individual relationships formed, as often the LA officers and heads had known each other for many years and also the extent to which each party needed the other. Heads generally enjoyed the greater balance of power in the relationship and knew they were being courted, as the LAs needed their skills. The expertise lay with the system leaders and not the LA. The heads had little sympathy for the reducing influence of LAs, as they believed that they had allowed schools to fail in their locality and so to some extent deserved their loss of power in the system.

The extent to which the LA supported the heads who undertook school-to-school support differed widely depending on circumstances from considerable support for some executive heads to others, usually in federations, who had little or no additional contact for support. In brokering school improvement services, LAs were acting like an agency for school services, which is a situation more likely to develop as Teaching Schools grow in number and influence. There was a mixed reaction from LAs regarding academy conversion. Some heads reported a hostile attitude, whereas others reported that the LAs accepted the position and even offered support. This appeared to depend on the size and capacity of the LA. With a small sample it is only possible to speculate but it would seem that LAs which had already commissioned out most of their improvement work were less possessive about retaining schools.

Relationships with National College

The majority of heads accessed work which was directly related to programmes or opportunities which involved the National College. These were manifested either directly through employment as facilitators on programmes, acting as consultant leaders or as part of working groups. In addition, NLEs and LLEs are validated through the college even though their work is brokered through the LA. In monitoring the work of NLEs, determining their continued status and designating teaching schools, National College exerts considerable control over this aspect of the system.

The strategic role of the headteacher and the development of new roles for staff

The heads were highly strategic in the way in which they used their understanding of the skills and abilities of staff and distributed leadership to manage their own roles and their schools as organizations. This strategy was undertaken to enable heads to manage:

- The work intensification they encountered as part of the increases in bureaucracy by implementing government policy.
- Their pursuit of other roles both internal and external.

Headteachers undertook to build capacity in one or more schools in three ways by:

- Creating new roles for staff
- Distributing leadership
- Creating a more strategic and less, or changing, operational role for themselves

Creating new roles for teaching staff

Workforce reform was used as a mechanism by heads to create new roles or change existing ones to build capacity to manage their own role. A change in terminology developed; for example, some heads referred to senior staff as 'directors' (Ht 12). Generally, however, heads followed a traditional hierarchy in their use of SLTs, which consisted of a variation of deputy and assistant headships and TLRs 1 and 2. Executive heads also introduced a non-traditional role into schools which they all referred to as 'head of school'. For most schools, however, the hierarchical structure for teachers was little changed in terms of *types* of role. What had changed was the *number* of these roles in some schools and *how* they were used in schools as heads employed this strategy to sustain capacity in the long term.

All heads praised their senior leaders for the way they could be relied upon to manage the school in their absence. One consequence of this is that much of the teaching role of deputies had reduced to allow them to undertake their increased role of school management. In addition, heads frequently undertook staffing restructures. Their motives were not only to improve internal management systems but also directly to manage their own absence as system leaders.

New roles for administrative support staff

Heads were using the role of support staff such as personal assistants and administrative staff to reduce their bureaucratic workload enabling them to lead more strategically. A school business manager (SBM) or equivalent was employed by 60 per cent of heads. They were frequently members of the SLT and were often working across schools particularly in long-term collaborations or federations. The SBM managed much of what was the chief executive role of the headteacher with responsibility for operational decision-making for premises and personnel, together with line managing non-teaching staff.

Of note is that all these SBMs were employed in two or more form entry schools. Southworth (2008) considered it necessary to have schools of at least 250 for a SBM to be affordable and if not for the cost to be shared between schools. With the exception of Ht 23's federation, none of the smaller schools in this study shared an SBM and all felt the burden of administration.

New roles for staff with ECM

While not being entirely sure what the extended schools agenda would look like in the early days of the interview schedule, there was an assumption by most of the heads in the first round that it 'would come to us' to manage (Ht 7), resulting in an 'intensification of our workload', which 'could be disastrous' (Ht 3). This, as much as for any other reason, was why most of them discussed taking an early decision to plan strategically for the requirements for extended schools through workforce reform by creating roles for staff to manage them.

Staff changes to take responsibility for ECM were implemented which included in several cases creating directors of ECM or assistant headships, together with the employment of managers of Children's centres. Two heads had employed managers for Children's Centres which were still virtual.

Building capacity: distributed leadership

Distributing leadership is a recognized strategy for building capacity (Spillane, 2006; Harris, 2008) and developing and retaining staff. Heads also used it for securing opportunities to be strategic with their own wider roles. While retaining staff may be a consequence of distributing leadership, it was not considered by the interviewees to be a main reason for the retention of staff, due to difficulties in recruitment. Heads believed that, due to the reputation of their schools and the opportunities for CPD in working across schools, they had little difficulty in recruiting staff.

Distributing leadership and offering new roles to staff required the heads to have the skills to manage change. They noted that care needed to be taken in building capacity. They were careful in changing the roles or responsibilities of staff that the good practice was not put at risk by staff working innovatively or being stretched. Heads recognized that a balance needed to be struck between their own role as a leader and the need to distribute leadership and empower and trust others. The argument lies in the extent to which the leadership of the roles was distributed, that is, the degree of responsibility; autonomy, authority and associated accountability were devolved and shared against the extent to which the tasks were merely delegated.

Despite the promotion of leadership for staff, there was some discrepancy between distributing leadership and accountability and delegating the management or operational role of the headteacher without corresponding decision-making power. Some heads felt they needed to keep a close, if more detached, eye on things. The main reasons given for this were that standards might drop, and that the head would lose overall control of the school. Most heads, however, identified that the leadership skills of staff were being enhanced by opportunities to lead school improvement in different contexts. Staff in supported schools also benefited from system leadership, as they were trained alongside staff in the base school. In federations, there were further opportunities to be redeployed for professional development. The relationship between the role of head and the extent to which they distributed leadership changed when heads employed a head of school. Neither they nor the staff expected the role of head to have the same degree of operational control.

An important aspect of this finding is that, although heads who had a new role may have practised the use of distributed leadership, few heads were actually *doing* it and genuinely 'letting go' (Ht 17) until the new roles took them away from their schools and they had to distribute leadership to manage and maintain the schools' success. Therefore, the heads were not necessarily distributing leadership by *choice* but by *necessity*.

While heads felt that staffs needed to 'endorse the absence of the head' (Ht 12) for other extended roles, there is some evidence that staffs had to be 'persuaded' (Ht 19). I am mindful of the question posed by Bottery (2004, 21), 'What if those in formal positions don't wish to have their power redistributed'? This is potentially damaging to a system which relies on the distribution of power through collaboration both in terms of the headteacher relinquishing operational power and for the SLTs who themselves have relinquished some operational power to middle leaders and, in turn, to teaching support staff. Without the views of the staffs concerned, further debate is outside the scope of this book.

The strategic and operational role of the headteacher

Some heads were still engaged in the teaching and learning process in one or more schools, despite having an extended role. They gave four reasons why:

- Some heads wished to prove to their staff they still had the skills to manage planning and monitor a curriculum area.
- It depended on the extent to which schools had a sufficiently large budget to pay for the staff needed. In small schools, there was evidence it hadn't, leading to heads having a more operational role such as that of Headteachers 9, 25 who were the SENCO but through necessity and not choice.
- It depended on the work intensification caused by the demands of new roles and the limit to the amount of work headteachers could undertake themselves.
- It depended on the importance heads attached to their being the lead learner to ensure the school/s delivered on performance of the standards. Failure to do so was seen to jeopardize the security and capacity of their schools, seen as essential to maintain if they were to have the credibility to pursue other work.

That heads were working across schools or had a more intensified work role within a single school meant they had to find different ways of monitoring standards and performance. This led to an increase in the use of senior managers in the production of curriculum and other audit reports. Nevertheless, heads were still heavily involved in managing and leading the process. Even executive heads with heads of school were operationally involved with their SLT in the monitoring and evaluation audits of their schools.

Performance management involving the use of team leaders has also enabled heads to be more strategic in monitoring the performance of staff and many now used it as a 'celebration' (Ht 12) of staff's achievement. Nevertheless, some heads still felt there was a need to undertake some of the monitoring themselves. Different reasons were given, including a lack of trust in the team to do it, context such as taking over a school in an OFSTED category, inclination and style, or necessity due to lack of time. While the reputation of heads is so crucially bound up with inspection of the performance of schools, it is unlikely that they will leave this aspect of leadership to chance and, so, trust is limited by pragmatism.

Power and centrality of headteachers

Heads were central to their organizations. They weren't letting go of power but putting in structures to lead from a distance but not to lead less. In spite of a degree of trust and distributed leadership, the school's direction followed the head's view of how it should be developed and should react to the educational agenda. A collective vision was often achieved through consensus but, nevertheless, because of the power of the head, albeit one removed and pushed through the use of SLTs, all the headteachers ultimately controlled the distribution of leadership and degree of autonomy enjoyed by others (Hatcher, 2005).

Adapting leadership styles to manage new roles and build capacity

The complexity of leadership styles

While heads had very different personalities and worked in different contexts, they were charismatic following the criteria laid down by House (1977, in Fidler and Atton, 2004). They tended to dominate the agenda, needed to influence others and had strong conviction regarding the integrity of their beliefs. They expressed high ideals for the success of the organizations and confidence in the staff to follow these ideals. While they had some freedom at the margins, they were also, in common with the findings of Bush (2008a), simultaneously constrained to work within centrally determined policies.

Leadership style depended on context and the extent of power, control and influence associated with the role. There is strong supporting evidence that heads were able to sustain success in more than one school due to their understanding of 'contingent leadership' (Leithwood et al., 2007) and management of change. The evidence is not just anecdotal but based also on that of OFSTED, which shows that schools have been removed from category or likely to be removed shortly according to HMI interim reports, as a result of the intervention of the system leadership of 12 of the headteachers.

Leadership styles, system leadership and control

Consultancy roles across schools were essentially 'client led', often with an existing substantive headteacher and short term. In these circumstances, system leaders needed to operate through influence which called for sensitivity and reliance on good relationships and cooperation. Setting the direction of schools was more likely if the role was formal and long term and brokered by the LA when the supported school had failed. Heads were given a degree of transferred authority from the LA and, so, autonomy and power to act. With the presence of an acting or substantive headteacher in the client school, heads had slightly less control, but the understanding given by the LAs was always that the final decision rested with the system leader, though the authority of that was less-overtly expressed.

The highest level of control and influence lay with those who were heads of long-term collaborations and federations and had overall responsibility for the leadership of the school. Leadership style was linked to the sustainability of the collaborative arrangement. Initially, when setting up systems, heads drove improvement from the front and used their personal power to establish effective systems and working relationships. However, they became more collegiate as the situation changed and schools became more independent.

Heads were acting in a form of collegiate leadership and trust if staff were working towards the school's values, aims and priorities. However, there is evidence that they would become authoritarian if members of staff were not. It is difficult to be specific with examples because none of the heads reported any form of real opposition and it was outside the scope of this book to find out the views of other members of staff. Therefore, it is not possible to argue if the collaborative style of heads had led to a form of 'contrived collegiality' (Hargreaves, 2001).

Leadership practice and system leadership

Heads used opportunities afforded by workforce reform to be flexible in the way roles were deployed or created across schools, as the following examples illustrate:

- Teaching and non-teaching staff deployed across schools.
- A chosen future successor acting as an apprentice and 'practising' (Ht 21) the job, particularly in the absence of the head.
- Opportunity at different tiers of leadership 'acting up' in the absence of the headteacher for part of the week either formally or informally.
- The creation of heads of school to undertake the leadership of a single school as part of a federation with an executive head.

There was a tendency for the heads in executive headteacher positions to treat the schools they worked with as branches of one organization with similar entitlements. However, within this broad approach, heads also differentiated for the needs of each school. A typical example was when another head described how she might offer 'a watered-down version' (Ht 19) of an initiative for the client school, but in contrast when staff in the client school showed particular skill, she also used them in training others. Another example is when a head of a federation moved many of the staff from a vulnerable school to build capacity in a family of schools made possible through the imposition of federation contracts.

Capacity could be built effectively as staffs were moved around schools in a federation and, therefore, able to learn quickly from a variety of contexts. Promotion can be attained from within the federation, as there is opportunity within a number of schools. Heads were talent spotting in one school or in a federation and growing the leadership of staff for internal promotion.

The ability to manage change

Effective management of change is generally accepted as being a characteristic of effective leadership. These heads, however, were not just managing imposed change but actively seeking new roles and challenges. There were five reasons for this:

- Their experience, style and characteristics as headteachers allowed them to sift and prioritize what was best for their schools and their leadership without being diverted by other policy agendas,

- There was more opportunity to shape their roles as they wished, due to the increased 'flexibility' in the system (Chapman et al., 2008) coupled with the fact that, at times, they were working in circumstances the system had not yet micro-managed.
- They recognized that new roles could be beneficial both for their schools and for their own careers by developing their professional expertise.
- They took the opportunity through workforce reform and the precedent it set for shaping staffing to suit the needs of the school to create the workforce which suited best the direction of the head and schools.
- They distributed leadership with greater autonomy and responsibility and trusted staff more. However, in trusting them more, there was identification of a corresponding need for tighter strategic level monitoring of the performance of staff and standards of pupil attainment.

A degree of autonomy allowed the heads the freedom to act quickly as the situation demanded and the evidence shows that they had the ability and courage to do so. They needed to be able to prioritize and plan ways of managing the agenda while maintaining their position in the market by ensuring their school's rating in the OFSTED hierarchy. They either shaped policy deliberately themselves to suit their circumstances as in workforce reform, or they addressed successfully the unintended consequences of policy which had created tension in the agenda. There was a similarity in the way in which these heads viewed leadership in terms of accountability and the desire to seek new opportunities and how they managed change, which transcended differences between them in terms of school context.

The effects of accountability on the actions and reactions of headteachers

Accountability for standards

The issue of standards was identified as being relentless and permeated the actions of the heads in all they undertook. Decisions about curriculum, how to deploy staff, and their own strategic role and new roles were all taken with a consideration of their impact on standards in the school. For some heads, this created a dilemma and led to a trade-off with balancing the best interests of the children's education and well-being while maintaining standards and, consequently, the reputations of themselves and their schools.

Another dilemma was managing children's special educational needs along with the need to maintain standards. Some of the issues were lack of funding for ECM and SEN initiatives, and the inclusion of children with severe behavioural difficulties in mainstream. These issues permeated different contexts and were neither solely a rural nor an urban problem or one purely for those in circumstances serving economic deprivation. None of the heads disagreed with the principle of including children with SEN but did wish to have a system of fair accountability so that the tensions in the agenda and the issues of funding were recognized.

Accountability and the heads' role

There was general agreement by heads that they should be accountable for the performance of their schools. Many believed that the arrangements pre-OFSTED were too ad hoc and open to systemic problems of lack of consistency of practice across schools. While accepting accountability through OFSTED as a given, heads departed from any general approval when considering the fairness of its application. Concern was expressed that inspectors were too reliant on data determined pre-inspection, together with its perceived lack of accuracy.

Throughout these interviews, heads were discussing self-evaluation in the same terms as self-inspection and, in doing so, they were 'translating' the 'protocols' of OFSTED and using them as an 'audit' for pre-inspection (MacBeath, 2008, 138). Even when the expectation to use the SEF was removed (DfE, 2010b), the need for self-evaluation as a means of preparing for inspection remained and, so, something similar to the SEF was still used.

Most heads weren't concerned with short-notice inspections because of the need to be on constant alert because they expected to fail. However, to manage the process they needed to be in school. Short notice meant that as system leaders in other schools this would be more difficult to ensure, engendering a degree of insecurity for some. It could be claimed that if leadership is distributed and the systems in school are robust, it doesn't matter if the head is in school or not for the inspection. While acknowledging the logic of this view, it misses the point that heads feel they have an obligation to support their staff through the trauma of inspection as well as needing to keep an eye on proceedings.

Heads managed the process of inspection not just to secure the school but also to gain validation as leaders to pursue wider roles. For the majority of these heads, stress over inspection was affected by the paradox of their gaining recognition. Heads may have resented OFSTED because of the way they were forced to comply with nationally mandated change, but they also needed it as a reference to enhance their careers.

Data and assessment

Elmore (2005) recognized the importance of school leaders building internal capacity in schools to offset the demands of accountability by situating themselves well to manage its demands. One of the most important ways they did that was to ensure the data sets the school up for success. Hence, the increased sharpened focus on performance management and focus on school leadership to deliver pupil progress against measurable criteria (Husbands, 2001). The ability to read, assess and manipulate data was seen as crucial particularly with OFSTED's increasing reliance on them. Due to this factor and their place in inspection and in SIPs' evaluations, the accuracy of the system for analyzing data at all levels becomes critical.

Many heads identified the perceived unfairness of the accuracy of marking. The situation reached a height in 2008 with the marking debacle, which culminated in the sacking of the company responsible for testing. Around 50 per cent of heads commented on the importance of ensuring accuracy of the attainment of children in Year 2 and their progress in Year 6 as identified by the SATs. Heads resented that they had to show the progress of their schools at the end of Year 6, compared with a time when the 'goal posts were different' (Ht 11) in Year 2. They highlighted that they needed to take 'brave' (Ht 12) action to rectify the problems created not by them but an imperfect system, which reacted with little discretion and was predicated more on 'the luck of the draw with inspectors' (Ht 8) than on being well designed as a system of accountability.

Performativity and stress

All heads felt under varying degrees of pressure to perform to secure the expected standards of performance of the children, and validation of their leadership through inspection. If inspection was successful, it dealt with the accountability of the headteacher to stakeholders because they would be secure in the knowledge that the standards and performance of the school were at an expected or satisfactory level. Heads who had led schools and achieved a judgement of outstanding or good with outstanding features from OFSTED experienced a high level of autonomy.

It was important, therefore, to manage the impression (Webb, 2006) gained by external assessors of the schools data and to choose it carefully remembering 'less is more' (Ht 12). However, for 30 per cent of the heads, despite their previous successes, the self-evaluation system still created fear and concern as they felt that their data didn't set them up for an outstanding judgement in inspection. Therefore, heads could be under stress due to the danger of losing high profile reputations as system leaders.

The personality of some heads drove them to improve their schools continually because they were worried that they would 'never be good enough' (Ht 9) or would get 'found out' (Ht 23). Despite this fear, heads generally had high levels of personal control which allowed them to cope. Some were working in very stressful situations, such as Ht 13, who was working in two schools. One of which was in special measures and was undergoing the removal of its governing body and in the other she was required to set up a Children's Centre. Another had to accept considerable opposition from some parent governors and the LA when setting up an academy (Ht 22). However, the stress is short lived and a key feature of these heads is their resilience and ability to manage pressure and change. All the heads in this research, while suffering stress at times, still had a high enough degree of professional self-efficacy to be able to cope with it.

The drug of leadership

Gronn (2003) noted that school leaders became addicted to the job and found it all consuming. In addition to this, I found that the heads were often overwhelmed by the intensity of their work but nevertheless they were choosing to find more intensified work and more challenging system leadership roles. These roles were voluntary and to some extent temporary and so heads could choose to remove themselves should they wish to. However, they enjoyed working with high levels of pressure and needed the sense of achievement they experienced when working in difficult situations. Heads' responses suggest that leadership is addictive and acts like a drug on its dependents, who suffer from this addiction with the consequences of needing to be constantly performing and can't manage without the 'buzz' it brings.

Evidence of earned autonomy and heads implementing government policy

Glatter (2006, 71) noted the attitude of government towards 'vision' that you can have 'any vision you like so long as it fits with ours'. The extent to which the direction of the schools was a product of the heads' own vision or that of the government is debatable and varied in this study in range and extent.

It was the intention of the government to allow those heads validated through inspection judgements a degree of earned autonomy to make decisions regarding the direction of their schools. However, is that true? Can autonomy operate if the choices over which it is exercized are limited by government policy? To what extent have heads internalized the need for government policy? Heads may support policy not because of pragmatism but because the government has been successful in persuading them of the need for it. An example is those heads that actively supported the need for OFSTED as a mechanism for being held to account rather than, for example, a form of democratic accountability, or believe in the setting of targets for children's test performance for staff because it is 'for the children' (Ht 13).

MacBeath (2008, 141) argued, 'By virtue of their office, heads have the freedom to decide, or impose, ways of working'. However, this is a bounded freedom because it is also acknowledged that there are constraints that heads have been found to be under in managing centrally imposed practice. Bush (2008, 284, original emphasis) argues, 'School leaders and managers are able to choose how to carry out a new policy but not *whether* to do so'. Heads determined how to implement policy and also, to a limited extent, whether to do so, and the evidence illustrates that heads will find ways of subverting or fully implementing policy, especially if 'surrounded by others sympathetic to their aims' (Bottery, 2007a, 158).

Earning autonomy by acting tactically

The extent to which heads could determine either how or whether to implement policy was precisely because of their success with government led outcomes and their securing a high performance for their school. This determined their validation as school leaders as, in turn, it led to outstanding OFSTED judgements and the freedom or earned autonomy this gave them to lead.

The element of risk is higher for the heads in this study, due to the importance of their reputations for their new and extended roles. The fall from grace through failure in inspection would be further, more public, and affect their ability to choose external roles. It is, therefore, essential that heads know which position to take when relating to government policy. Examples of them doing so can be supported by comments such as 'we all know how to play the game' (Ht 8) over presentation for OFSTED or becoming early academy converters to shape the agenda rather than have it shaped for them (Ht 22, Ht 23).

While acknowledging the idea that they were being granted earned autonomy, nevertheless heads were concerned about the 'fragility' of this autonomy (Ht 8), due to its dependence on their performance and that of their schools. They believed it to be a 'myth' because of the constraints of government policy (Ht 12), or that it was dependent on the vagaries of the governing body (Ht 3) and that many heads hadn't 'any faith in the reasons behind' (Ht 7) their being granted autonomy as being for anything other than achieving the required results in school tests and complying with government policy. The climate in which heads found themselves raised a question regarding the extent to which they were proactive and shaping the vision for their schools independently of externally mandated policy and the extent to which they were constrained and reactive. This question suggested the following options:

- The heads were acting independently and choosing whether to implement policy and know this as a form of resistance.
- They were acting as they thought independently but were actually only working within the parameters of government policy and tinkering around the edges of reform.
- They were aware that they were highly constrained but didn't fight it because of fear and were compliant or 'disturbed conformists' (Woods et al., 1997).
- They were strategically compliant (Moore et al., 2002) and implementing the national agenda in order to locate for themselves and their school a degree of earned autonomy.

Compliance, mediation and resistance

Bottery (2007a, 160, original emphasis) noted that if a 'culture of compliance' exists, then to alter it the government will have to 'change a culture of conformity *which it has created*'. To some extent, the Labour government tried to do so with the urging of schools to be creative in the design and implementation of the curriculum and the Coalition with its urging of schools to seek academy freedoms. This was making it easier for leaders to manage the government agenda but not for them to act outside it. It is difficult to find a pattern of response in that heads weren't consistent in whether or not they complied with policy as a general rule. Heads' actions were contingent on their own circumstances and those of their schools and their reactions dependent on which aspect of policy or expectations they were reacting and, in this, were showing a range of responses within compliance identified by Woods et al. (1997) as ranging from 'supporting' through 'surviving' to 'disturbed conformists'.

When the response of the heads could be *mediation* (Hoyle and Wallace, 2007, original emphasis) and they could adapt statutory policy, such as testing, in the best interests of their children, they did. However, heads became 'disturbed conformists' (Woods et al., 1997) when they were constrained by teaching to the test to protect their school but which then led to mediation to accommodate testing at Year 2 to survive in Year 6 and to be sure of showing expected progress. Any deviance was an act of 'principled infidelity' (Hoyle and Wallace, 2007), which was deemed acceptable, both as an act of survival and also because heads felt they were representing the truth in the only way they could.

They were independent regarding some pressures to conform from peers or associations. The NAHT invited heads to refuse to administer tests to children at the end of KS2 in 2010, although few in this study took action, despite some local pressure. They reasoned this was not because of fear of the consequences but because it was in the best interests of children who had worked hard to prepare for them, and while they were aware of the tests shortcomings, they prioritized the needs of the children as they perceived them, first.

Simultaneous compliance and resistance

To some extent, their response to legislation restricted heads' actions, as heads were sometimes reactive and not proactive towards policy, but the findings are more complicated than can be categorized by reverting to strategies encapsulated in an either/or definition of being proactive or reactive. They tried to create the context for learning and pedagogy and to locate a space for themselves by being strategically pragmatic. Heads responded to new opportunities in ways which enabled them as much as possible to be true to what they would see as their core purpose and to act with some independence where their compliance to the agenda had granted them success and some autonomy.

Heads managed the agenda strategically, as they knew their position gave them power. One head described informing governors 'after the event' due to the speed with which the agenda of the school needed to be implemented (Ht 19). Another, that she had the freedom to introduce programmes and initiatives as she thought fit in her client school 'unhindered' (Ht 13). This study indicates that it was not a question of heads either complying or not, but that they both resist and comply, often simultaneously (Thomson, 2008).

Changes to the role of heads, governors and the LA have implications for the school system. The power of the head has increased as the knowledge of the system becomes located in them. This is consistent over the period of the research but particularly as practice outpaces policy and system knowledge.

Implications and Recommendations for Government Policy

9

The Labour and Coalition governments have sought to drive their reforms to improve schools through the role and practice of headteachers. This has included their endorsement for the use of school-to-school support or system leadership. As the government cannot control the spread or effectiveness of system leadership through micro-managing it at national level, it remains important that the system is 'self improving' (Hargreaves, 2010) or self corrects. An analysis of the perceptions and opinions of the headteachers indicate that there are some implications for government and schools in using system leadership and school structural reform to raise standards and build capacity and sustainability in the system. These issues affect the following areas and form the basis for the subheadings and recommendations for government to consider:

- Using system leadership to effect change
  - Create the climate of interest in, and generate opportunities for, system leadership roles.
  - Create the conditions for sustainable system leadership.

- o Generate opportunities for CPD to encourage the recruitment and retention of system leaders.
- o Understand and manage the implications of leadership in an era of austerity.
- Diversity, fragmentation and the role of the middle tier
  - o Create the conditions to manage the deployment of system leaders in a diverse system.
  - o Understand the implications of introducing diversity into the school system.
  - o Manage the tension between competition and collaboration.
- The role of accountability
  - o Improve the reliability of data and consistency of inspection judgements.
  - o Ensure a balance between earned autonomy and accountability.
  - o Create the conditions for judgements to be made about leadership and partnership across schools.
- The changing role of governance
  - o Improve the understanding of their role, quality and consistency of governors.
  - o Manage the implications of the changes to the role of governors as a result of its reforms.

Using system leadership to effect change

Create the climate of interest in, and generate opportunities for, system leadership roles

While there may be the permission and active encouragement by government for system leadership, it needs to ensure there are opportunities for headteachers to access, which has implications for the system's knowledge of where the need and capacity exists. The role of the National College is crucial in this regard, as it designates NLEs and LLEs and evaluates the effectiveness of their system leadership (Hill and Matthews, 2008; 2010). Sustainability of school-to-school support is dependent on individual localities having the capacity in their schools to use heads in this way, and those heads having the will and motivation to be used. This is further complicated by the quality of the match of each school and of the evaluation of the process and the extent to which each party is flexible, willing and able to adapt to changing needs. The findings suggest heads are motivated by moral purpose but not at the expense of their own reputation or their schools place in any organizational hierarchy.

Create the conditions for sustainable system leadership

Heads agreed that school-to-school support through various forms of collaboration is effective because the provision is bespoke and locality driven by those who understand the context in which they are working. It is important, therefore, that government recognizes and creates the conditions for sustainable system leadership. Federations which are largely permanent are more likely to be sustainable organizations. However, there could be an issue of managing succession due to the level of sophisticated leadership skills needed to undertake the leadership of two or more schools successfully. Many heads dealt with this before it became a concern by training senior staff from within their organization to take over. Heads may be sustaining capacity in their own federation, but doing so has implications for the spread of expertise across the school system.

More difficult is the sustainability of improvement in short-term consultancies or collaborations, both in terms of the capacity of the base school sustaining the number of system leaders needed, and the client school's sustainability if or when the system leader exits. The intention was that the client school should be able to support itself once system leadership support had ceased. Despite this, involvement with the client school is dependent on the interest and whim of the system leader. This has clear implications for sustainability of improvement and the roles of others, as the supported school could be left in an even more vulnerable situation once the system leader has moved on. A complication is generated by the development of inter-school systems, which make sustainability more likely but 'untangling' (Ht 20) the results of collaboration in terms of relationships and roles more difficult. This applies to system leadership generally, and particularly executive headship, should schools wish, or are required, to revert back to single institutions.

Success was viewed as more likely by the headteachers if there was a seconded or executive headteacher who has the power to make real and sustained change in the most vulnerable schools. This shouldn't lead to a diminished role for CLs, but merely affect their deployment. The role of NLEs is specifically to work in schools most at risk of failure, and the use of the support school is an important element in sustaining improvements and using a greater spread of expertise to do so. There are, however, different degrees of need and the use of CLs in the short term or for less-vulnerable schools can still lead to improvement. Notwithstanding all of this, the short-term nature of external involvement will almost inevitably lead to problems of sustainability, possibly caused by the extent to which system leaders are stretched across several schools. This is arguably what the concept of schools working in long-term collaborations and federations is meant to address.

Generate opportunities for CPD to encourage the recruitment and retention of system leaders

Some successes, such as co-locating schools, chains of schools or academies together with ways of working, such as consultancy, can be replicated. To be effective across the system, such practice should be evaluated through research. It should include the impact of context, established as valid, and then communicated through professional development and opportunities. This would facilitate the transfer of knowledge and ideas that are considered to be effective and innovative in one school for the benefit of the system and reduce school failure. Both as a result of this research and as an experienced head who undertakes system leadership, I think building capacity through a menu of opportunities gives heads the necessary understanding of what is needed in these complex situations of system leadership. I believe it is not a coincidence, for example, that a majority of the heads had undertaken primary strategy consultant leadership (PSCL) under the PLP programme or other consultant leadership training such as London Challenge or the National College before moving on to further system leadership or extended roles.

This has important implications for the training and development of future school leaders to offer not just national programmes with competency-based training but also other forms of training and development. These need to include practical opportunities to gain experience in the field in small bespoke school-to-school and other collaborations. Much of the training for future system leaders stems from experience gained as a leader in a support school. One unintended consequence is that using staff across federations is undoubtedly successful in terms of building local capacity. However, there is a potential issue in that practice is becoming locked into schools and collaborations, both in the maintained sector and in sponsored chains. Teachers are gaining experience and opportunities across federations, but this isn't necessarily spreading expertise across the system. There is potential for those schools which cannot offer these opportunities to fail to recruit and potentially create a two-tier system.

Understand and manage the implications of leadership in an era of austerity

Schools have been used to working collaboratively according to the pressures of the extended schools agenda and it is likely that with the reduction in school support services this will expand. Such collaboration has taken advantage of economies of scale and opportunities otherwise not open to them, as well as being an access route to grants. To some extent, there is no option in this form of collaboration. However, there is a choice to undertake collaborating with schools to support them to make improvements to practice, which may have implications for them continuing.

School-to-school support through local authorities and the NLE programme has been well supported financially for many heads. However, this climate changed with the recession and the Coalition government introduced its strategies, promising a new age of austerity. To what extent the successes of system leadership have depended on the increased funding levels of the Labour government will become apparent. However, system leadership and building capacity doesn't come without cost. Most heads commented that enabling others to act up or to lead across schools and build capacity was dependent on having sufficient funding. Most heads will wish to support colleagues, but with funding difficulties may have to find new ways of doing so. At the very least, it will require an increase in collaborations and networks to gain economies of scale, but teaching schools and collaborative working will still incur capacity costs. A lack of funding will impact on their effectiveness and the depth and breadth of the support they offer to other schools.

Diversity, fragmentation and the role of the middle tier

Create the conditions to manage the deployment of system leaders

The effectiveness of system leadership depends on the extent to which they are deployed and this is largely at the behest of LAs, which have brokered system leaders to support vulnerable schools. Being dependent on local negotiation makes role availability disjointed and fragmented and has implications for national policy, as the system at the national level has less control over the process and 'its replication' (Chapman et al., 2008). The abolition of SIPs, infrequent OFSTED inspections and increase of schools opting out of local authority control will contribute to decreasing LAs' knowledge of school capacity in their area. This might be made worse as the local system diversifies with school structural reform, and the number of system leaders available for deployment outside those known to National College will be increasingly difficult to calculate. If the local system is slow to react to need, there is a danger that some schools could slip through the net and fail before they are picked up. The government needs to consider how to manage the *distance* in the system, potentially worsened by diversity, between the system leaders and the government's intention that they are used. Failure to do so could make into ghettos those areas of failing schools and systematize failure.

Understand the implications of introducing diversity into the school system

The role of the school as an organization is changing. There are developing different local systems, which can include sponsored chains, federations, free schools, faith schools community schools and others. This is introducing more choice in the market for parents, which it is believed will drive schools to self improve. It doesn't necessarily follow, however, that school structural change leading to more diversity in the system will lead to improvements in outcomes for children or better leadership.

Breaking the pattern or cycle of endemic failure in schools by fundamentally changing systems can begin the process of improvement. Failing schools can and have benefited from partnerships with successful schools, which have sometimes rapidly removed staff, changed the focus and ethos of the schools, and introduced known working operational systems. Innovation can drive or be a lever for school improvement, but if the freedom to create new school structures and chains leads to poor quality outcomes for children, it will be more difficult to discern as the system fragments.

If chains of schools become an increasingly large part of the middle tier replacing much of the role of LAs, then will who will gather and disseminate the knowledge of effective practice in the system? There is no guarantee that chains will do so beyond their own schools. It needs to be a priority for government as there is a potential that, having unleashed innovation, they will fail to profit by it if they lack the mechanisms to gather information about it or transfer it. The transfer of knowledge across the system argued as important for school improvement could be lessened, not expanded, by a more diverse and less-managed school system.

There are many countries which do not have national systems but rely on states or districts. However, a national system of education delivered at local district and school level has been one of the hallmarks of the English system. Will there be disadvantages to planning across the whole system with increased localism? One danger in losing national knowledge is how the government will plan and manage the number of initial teacher trainees it needs if teacher training is determined locally (Ryan, 2011).

What role will school context play in a more diverse system? The Coalition has based much of its policy over what worked in urban environments, especially London and the other National Challenge areas. It needs to ensure that it replicates this in other contexts, most notably in rural areas. The implications of free schools should be researched to determine if they are unleashing unfair competition into the system as they compete for resources. If some schools grow at the expense of others, what will happen to those which can't compete? Will they close and fail or be taken over by nearby successful schools? One difficulty for government is that places are unlikely to be available in successful local schools, as the birth rate increases putting pressure on the system.

Successive governments have wanted to ensure that those children with the least social capital are able to thrive in the education system. Potentially, however, these children will be more vulnerable in a destabilized system if the quasi-market isn't successful in determining a match of need to provision. What about those children whose parents don't understand the system and don't make wise and informed choices for their children's education? In addition, while accepting that there is the opportunity for parents to open schools under the free school system, it is questionable that the quasi-market can respond quickly enough to provide for demand.

Manage the tension between competition and collaboration

Competition may help to create impetus for self-improvement, but this does not necessarily translate into effective collaboration. Will the competition in the system between schools for admissions, league tables and so on allow the collaboration needed for a self-improving system? Removing the controls of the LA won't in itself mean that heads will become more inclined towards localism and collaboration.

It is difficult to predict the speed of growth of federations or chains of schools in each locality or, consequently, what their impact will be on the role of LAs or networks of schools. One consideration, however, is the difference in attitude to collaboration between sponsored chains with different heads and federations which employ the same executive head. There is an expectation that schools collaborate across the chain, but what will be the drivers and incentives for them to collaborate with schools outside their chain? Will other schools want to collaborate with these potentially closed organizations?

Local authorities will still be expected to monitor school's performance but will have decreasing resources to do so. Therefore, it will be important for networks of schools and federations to work together to provide the intelligence to identify issues of vulnerability in other schools. If a head is leading a federation, they will have the intelligence, power and authority to monitor, evaluate and put in improvement strategies. However, even if they are aware of the vulnerability in neighbouring schools, will they publicly acknowledge this and identify issues in schools for which they don't have a direct responsibility? This is a much more interventionist approach for heads than being brokered to find solutions already identified by others. What will be their authority for doing so if the substantive head of a school in difficulties chooses not to access help? The system can't correct unless there is power to do so.

If teaching schools are expected to identify the need for support in its network of schools, I think heads will respond and do so. However, the issues here are firstly that there is no insistence that other schools join a teaching school network. Secondly, in the interim until enough teaching schools have been identified and established, the existing reduction in the role and local knowledge of the LA could cause schools to fail unnoticed until too late. However, as several heads were quick to point out, schools have been failing under the system where LAs had a role in school improvement and so their variable quality and capacity will determine the extent to which their role in this context is missed. Thirdly, as school-to-school support relies on the willingness of heads to collaborate, the power dynamics lie with them. However, this will change with NLEs working with teaching schools. Some consideration needs to be given by government as to what happens to the brokerage and work of partnerships, particularly teaching school partnerships, if the parties disagree. Will they be easy to disassemble, and what will be the consequences if they do?

The role of accountability

Improve the reliability of data and consistency of inspection judgements

Part of the importance of attracting effective headteachers is due to their centrality in the system. They are the ones on whom the government relies to implement its policy successfully and so they need to be chosen and assessed carefully and accurately. One way of doing so is to rely on inspection results for schools and the performance of the children in tests. Unfortunately, this has been found to be a flawed system due to inaccuracies of marking tests and the formulaic way 'outstanding' is determined as a judgement. An example of the former is the debacle around the marking of SATs 2008 when the company responsible was sacked. Frustration regarding testing continued until some heads boycotted them in 2010. An example of the latter can be cited with reference to schools which were deemed to be outstanding by OFSTED due to the high levels of CVA achieved but considered to be failing by the DCSF because they were attaining below the targets for passes at GCSE for A–Cs. The reduced framework implemented from September 2011 will have the same systemic disadvantages if it relies on inconsistent judgements and data.

Ensure a balance between earned autonomy and accountability

A further complication is that the dependence on inspection to validate heads was partly removed by the Coalition. They sought to strengthen the earned autonomy of schools already begun by Labour in removing outstanding schools from inspection and using interim assessments to defer the inspection of good schools. However, there are several potential difficulties arising from this action. If schools aren't to be inspected regularly, then how will the system know that the outstanding or good judgement is still valid? The use of desktop analysis will give information about performance but that is only one aspect of inspection.

OFSTED also relies on the level of parental complaint to make interim desktop assessments about schools. However, this will also create a delay in identifying failing schools, as I suspect it will take a long time before parents become fully aware of issues if schools choose to hide them. In addition, if there are no inspections for outstanding schools, how will inspectors know what outstanding looks like in terms of teaching and leadership and so learn to judge it and use that judgement to make comparisons with other practice (Ryan, 2011)? The effectiveness of inspection as a factor in determining those suitable for system leadership is diminished, therefore, if there is some disquiet over the validity and breadth of its judgements.

Create the conditions for judgements to be made about leadership and partnership across schools

Detecting failure is more difficult across schools when they are inspected singly rather than as a federation. It is logistically very difficult in large federations when so much of the process revolves around the leadership of the headteacher, who can't be in two places at once if schools are inspected simultaneously. The government needs to create the conditions for the system to evolve, with inspection becoming sophisticated and sensitive enough to make judgements about the leadership of heads across schools.

Headteachers are clearly accountable for the performance of the schools they lead but to what extent should they also be accountable for their partnerships with other schools? Inspection across schools is more complicated if there is introduced a system of locality accountability for partnership working across schools for heads who lead the partnerships such as teaching schools but do not have executive headship responsibilities over the schools in the group. They may be understandably resistant or reluctant to be held to account for the performance of other schools in their groups, over which they may not have direct control.

NLEs are brokered to work with underachieving schools and those in category. Good schools by definition don't need school-to-school support for vulnerability, but those schools that are just satisfactory are vulnerable and shouldn't slip through the net because the system is unable to detect them in time. With fewer interim measures to detect failing performance, such as SIPs or LA monitoring, it is important that the government recognizes triggers and detects any slippage in the performance of schools overall. OFSTED visits satisfactory schools more frequently, but government needs to ensure this is enough to manage any slippage in performance in the short term. In the long term, government may rely on teaching schools' networks to monitor and support its own schools. Will it also rely on individual chains to do the same, especially if they are not part of a teaching school network? What accountability mechanism will there be to ensure these chains are successful not just according to data for each school but for their partnership?

The changing role of governance

Improve the understanding of their role, quality and consistency of governors

The varied quality of governing bodies in their ability to undertake their duties is an ongoing issue for the government as they rely on governors to some extent to enable system leadership to take place. Implications for government lie in the success of changing the structure of the governance system and encouraging them to understand how school-to-school collaboration benefits not just their own school but also the system. Training is one way, and so the remit of the National College (NC, 2011b) extended to include training for chairs of governors will be crucial.

Manage the implications of the changes to the role of governors as a result of its reform

The changes to governance which have occurred through school structural reform have reduced the number of governors needed, including that of parent governors, and there is no requirement for representatives from the LA. So, apart from being accountable to ensure legal compliance and pupil performance, the governing body, and through them the headteacher, have an increased level of power in the system. Parental dissatisfaction is a mechanism to manage quality of a school but it is more difficult for them to make informed decisions about schools if the number and influence of their representatives are reduced on the governing body. The government needs to be aware of the implications of this for the wider professional accountability of schools and headteachers and create opportunities to discover issues before it is too late.

If the governing body is unable to understand the educational agenda in enough depth, and the school is treated as 'light touch' by the LA, or in the case of academies has no involvement in the schools, it is possible for heads to create a space through earned autonomy where they can work with considerable independence, unhindered by accountability to the governing body. Unless governors are able to hold heads to account effectively, it could take some time for the system to catch up through the traditional routes of accountability especially with new school structures.

Conclusion

An issue for any government committed to 'a self improving system' (Hargreaves, 2010) is where to draw the line between freedom and control. Government needs to allow enough slack in the system for heads to work and solve the messy 'adaptive challenge' (Heifetz, 1994) of school improvement, but with sufficient checks and balances to enable all participants in the system to be assured that the schools are progressing and not following an unchecked 'slalom ride' (Ht 19) to failure.

Chapter 1 highlighted the importance of considering the complexity of the school system as a whole and interrelated system. Dangers of non-aligned policies were highlighted, which could, and often did, produce unintended consequences. The Labour government was criticised for its micro-management with the introduction of guidelines for many aspects of its policy which constrained the leadership of headteachers. However, from its second term in office, Labour increasingly advocated a more diverse system and earned autonomy for effective heads. The introduction of NLEs from 2006, and latterly LLEs, together with accredited school groups from 2009 are examples of this approach.

The same dilemma of balancing freedom and control faces the Coalition. Its approach is to continue Labour's policy of diversity in schooling but increase it through new structural reform together with the encouragement of system leadership (see Chapter 2). It is the belief of the Coalition that it is not their role to micro-manage the school system, but to allow competition and the quasi-market to drive school improvement. Government's intention is that parents using the increased data provided by OFSTED and the DfE will make informed decisions. By being less prepared to be involved in the process of school improvement, they are relying on the self-interest or moral purpose of schools, chains and federations to drive their reforms. Teaching schools leading local networks are to be the cornerstones of this approach.

It is too early to comment on the success of teaching schools for this book except that they will rely not only on the drive and skills of the teaching school leadership but also on the willingness of other local heads of good schools to engage with them. While teaching schools are emerging, there are an increasing number of maintained schools and private providers of school improvement packages entering the market for professional development. The increasingly diminished capacity of the LA and the possible strain on teaching schools and others to deliver the capacity the system needs may leave much of this work to those outside the school system.

School structural reform and the introduction of new players such as free schools and sponsored academies and chains have changed the relationship between the state and the school system. Among the heads there was a large amount of enthusiasm for working towards a freer, more diverse system, with more opportunities for the profession to lead innovation and collaboration. But it isn't certain that there will be enough potential system leaders with the expertise and interest to undertake the work and that knowledge can be transferred across all contexts. The government needs to ensure that it is not overcome by change leaving a vacuum in the system while capacity is built up to manage the fragmentation which is being generated.

Change is difficult to predict and therefore it must be a high-risk strategy to push so much diversity into the system so early without evaluations or checks for how effective the changes will be. There is no guarantee that schools won't use the changes for self-interest rather than collaborate in the interests of the wider system. There is a consequential danger that if the school system fragments unchecked, it may fail to save the most vulnerable with the least understanding of how to access the system. The governments aim of 'closing the gap' of attainment will be unsuccessful. While the Coalition has called for increased data on schools as a way of holding them to account, data only tell part of the story of a school's effectiveness, as the evidence from the headteachers in this study suggests.

Traditionally, headteachers led single schools and set their direction. This picture of headship is changing rapidly as heads undertake system leadership. An understanding of the current role of headteachers is complicated by new roles for them in sponsored organizations. Heads were keen to increase the size of federations under their executive leadership. However, leadership of schools in a sponsored chain was not an attractive prospect for them, due to a perceived reduction in their autonomy. If sponsored primary chains develop to a large extent then the autonomy of the professional to shape, their schools and the education in their network will be diminished by having to follow the systems developed away from it. This will create a new and different pattern of leadership in the system, which the government should ensure works for the benefit of children and not just the market.

Overall, heads pursued the aims as outlined by the statutory agenda and, to a large extent, government has secured them as 'implementers of its reforms' (Bottery, 2004). Nevertheless, it isn't a straightforward picture of heads being merely a conduit for government policy. If they were unthinkingly implementing it, they wouldn't have experimented with the curriculum (Ht 12) or extended workforce arrangements (Ht 23) or sought to extend government policy by refraining from converting to an academy until all those in the federation could do so (Ht 26). Specific change at local and institutional level wouldn't have taken place.

Headteachers are at the very least values-led pragmatists. However, there was no evidence that heads had undertaken any strategy which would risk them failing at the next inspection and lose their and their school's reputation. That they pursue government agenda is important because the government is not always aware of the impact of its policies and moves much slower than do the headteachers who are impatient for change. If the result is that practice has often mediated policy, the government needs to ensure that the direction of travel with policy interpretation is the one it intends.

There should be a strong commitment to ongoing leadership development. New patterns of leadership put a greater onus on having high-quality leaders than ever before. It is important not only for heads to understand evidence-based practice and how they can use it to lead their own schools, but also what is the meaning behind the making of education policy and the drivers behind and tensions within it. The greater knowledge practitioners have about the system, the more informed their choices can be about acting in the best interests of their schools and not just the successful implementation of government policy. In doing so, if government is truly prepared for the system to be self-improving and driven by the profession, it will be better equipped to do so.

Glossary

AHT	Assistant Headteacher
CL	Consultant Leader
CPD	Continuing Professional Development
CVA	Contextual Value Added
DCS	Directors of Children's Services
DCSF	Department for Children, Schools and Families
DfE	Department for Education
DfES	Department for Education and Skills
DES	Department for Education and Science
EiC	Excellence in Cities
ECM	Every Child Matters
EYFS	Early Years Foundation Stage
FSM	Free School Meals
GCSE	General Certificate of Secondary Education
GMB	General, Municipal, Boilermakers and Allied Trade Union
GP	General Practitioner
HMCI	Her Majesty's Chief Inspector
HMI	Her Majesty's Inspectors
LA	Local Authority*
LEA	Local Education Authority
LLE	Local Leader of Education
LMS	Local Management of Schools
LPSH	Leadership Programme for Serving Headteachers
NAHT	National Association of Headteachers
NASUWT	National Association of Schoolmasters and Union of Women Teachers**
NCSL	National College for School Leadership***
NC	National College for Leadership of Schools and Children's Services
NLE	National Leader of Education
NPQH	National Professional Qualification for Headship

NPQICL	National Professional Qualification in Integrated Centre Leadership
NQT	Newly Qualified Teacher
NSS	National Support School
NUT	National Union of Teachers
OFSTED	Office for Standards in Education
OECD	Organisation for Economic Cooperation and Development
PE	Physical Education
PER	Primary Evaluative Review
PLP	Primary Leadership Programme
PPA	Planning Preparation and Assessment
PSCL	Primary Strategy Consultant Leader
QCA	Qualification and Curriculum Authority
QCDA	Qualifications and Curriculum Development Agency
QTS	Qualified Teacher Status
quangos	Quasi-non-governmental organizations
RIG	Rewards and Incentives Group
SBD	School Business Director
SBM	School Business Manager
SEF	Self Evaluation Form
SIO	School Improvement Officer (LA)
SIP	School Improvement Partner
SLE	Specialist Leader of Education
SLT	Senior Leadership Team
SSAT	Specialist Schools and Academies Trust
STRB	School Teachers Review Board
TA	Teaching Assistant
TDA	Training and Development Agency****
TTA	Teachers Training Agency
TES	Times Educational Supplement
TLR	Teaching and Learning Responsibility
WAMG	Workforce Agreement Monitoring Group

Notes

* LEAs became known as LAs during the course of the research as education was integrated as part of Children's Services following the Children's Act (2004). Participants in the research used the terms LA and LEA interchangeably as they were becoming more accustomed to the change of terminology.

** The NASUWT was shortened in the book by headteachers to NAS.

*** The National College for School Leadership changed its name following a change in remit in 2009, where it was required to undertake the training of Directors of Children's Services. It subsequently became The National College for Leadership of Schools and Children's Services, which is abbreviated to NC and referred to as The National College.

**** The Teacher Training Agency changed its name to the Training and Development Agency in 2005.

Appendix – Interview List of Headteachers

Headteacher (Ht)	Gender	Type of school	Number of pupils	Number of current headships held
1	Female	Urban	207	1
2	Female	Inner City	462	1
3	Female	Urban	384	1
4	Male	Inner City	183	1
5	Male	Inner City	654	1
6	Male	Rural	177	1
7	Male	Inner City	474	1
8 Revisit	Female	Inner City ditto	176 ditto	1 ditto
9	Female	Inner City	337	1
10	Female	Urban	383	1
11 Revisit	Male	Urban ditto	447 * 450, 200, 337	1 3
12	Female	Inner City	679	1
13 Revisit	Female	Inner City ditto	708 2* 700, 420	1 2
14 Revisit	Female	Urban ditto	360 ditto	1 ditto
15	Female	Inner City	382	1
16	Female	Inner City	621	1
17	Female	Urban	323	1
18	Female	Inner City	492	1
19 Revisit	Female	Inner City ditto	476, 600 3* 400, 570	2 2
20 Revisit	Female	Inner City ditto	669, 470 ditto	2 ditto
21	Male	Rural	250, 60	2
22	Female	Urban	260	1
23	Male	Rural	314, 95, 89, 73, 69	5
24	Female	Inner City	450, 200	2

Headteacher (Ht)	Gender	Type of school	Number of pupils	Number of current headships held
25	Female	Rural	55, 65	2
26	Male	Urban	4* 780, 400, 410	3
27	Male	Inner City	500, 380, 380	3

Notes

Headteachers Ht 5, Ht 7, Ht 8, Ht 9, Ht 14, Ht 17, were leading or collaborating with other schools, sometimes for part of the week, but were not officially recognized as executive heads at the time of interview.

* Ht 11 was executive head of a collaboration of three schools in the revisit, which consisted of his original base school from the first visit and the executive headship of two others added in the interim.

2* Ht 13 was still head of the same school in the revisit but had also been appointed head of a second school, becoming a federation.

3* Ht 19 was head of a two-school collaboration in the first visit. By the time of the revisit, she had become head of a different two-school federation.

4* Ht 26 was executive head of three schools in a federation of four schools.

Bibliography

Ackoff, R. L. (1974) *Redesigning the Future*. New York: Wiley.

Alexander, R. J. (ed.) (2010) *Children, Their World, Their Education: Final Report and Recommendations of the Cambridge Primary Review*. London: Routledge.

Ball, S. J. (1990) *Politics and Policy Making in Education*. London: Routledge.

—. (1998) Big policies/small world: An introduction to international perspectives in education policy, *Comparative Education* Vol. 34, No. 2, 119–130.

—. (2001) Performativities and fabrication in the education economy: Towards the performative society, in D. Gleeson and C. Husbands (eds), *The Performing School: Managing, Teaching, and Learning in a Performance Culture*. London: Routledge Falmer, 210–226.

—. (2003) The teacher's soul and the terrors of performativity, *Journal of Education Policy*, Vol. 18, No. 2, 215–228.

Barber, M. (2001) The very big picture, *School Effectiveness and School Improvement*, Vol. 12, No. 2, 213–228.

—. (2002) *The Challenge of Transformation*, Address for the Conference Series–Federal Reserve Bank of Boston. Available online www.bos.frb.org/economic/conf/conf47/conf47m.pdf. Accessed 30 April 2011.

—. (2005) *Informed Professionalism: Realizing the Potential*. Presentation to the Association of Teacher and Lecturers 11 June 20 2005.

Barber, M. and Fullan, M. (2005) *Tri-Level Development: It's the System*. Paper produced for publication *Education Week* (March). Available online www.michaelfullan.ca/Articles_05/Tri-Level%20Dev't.pdf. Accessed 4 January 2009.

Begley, P. (2009) Leading with moral purpose: The place of ethics, in Tony Bush, Les Bell and David Middlewood (eds), *The Principles of Educational Leadership and Management*, 2nd edn. London: Sage, 31–54.

Bell, L. (1999) Back to the future: The development of educational policy in England, *Journal of Educational Administration*, Vol. 37, No. 3, 200–228.

Bentley, T. (2002) Letting go: Complexity, individualism and the left, *Renewal*, Vol. 10. No. 1, 9–26.

—. (2003) Foreward in Hargreaves, D. H., *Education Epidemic: Transforming Secondary Schools through Innovation Networks*. London: Demos, 9–16.

Bolton, E. (1998) 'HMI—the Thatcher Years', *Oxford Review of Education*, Vol. 24, No. 1, 45–55.

Bottery, M. (2004) *The Challenges of Educational Leadership*. London: Sage.

—. (2006) Educational leaders in a globalising world: a new set of priorities? *School Leadership & Management*, Vol. 26, No. 1, 5–22.

—. (2007) New Labour policy and school leadership in England: Room for manoeuvre? *Cambridge Journal of Education,* Vol. 37, No. 2, 153–172.

Bryman, A (1992) *Charisma and Leadership in Organisations.* London: Sage.

Burns, J.A. (1978) *Leadership.* New York: Harper and Row.

Bush, T. (2003) *Theories of Educational Leadership and Management,* 3rd edn. London: Sage Publications.

—. (2008a) From management to leadership: Semantic or meaningful change? *Educational Management Administration and Leadership,* Vol. 36, No. 2, 271–288.

—. (2008b) *Leadership and Management Development in Education.* London: Sage.

—. (2010) Spiritual Leadership, *Educational Management and Administration,* Vol. 38, No. 4, 402–404.

Caldwell, B. and Paddock, S. (2008) Re-imagining schooling: Leadership voices, in Hopkins (ed.), *Transformation and Innovation: System Leaders in the Global Age.* Specialist Schools and Academies Trust. London, 103–127.

Callaghan, J. (1976) *The Prime Minister's Speech at Ruskin College, Oxford on Monday, 18 October 1976.* London: DfEE.

Carlson, R, (1965) Barriers to Change in Public Schools, in, R. Carlson et al. (eds), *Change Processes in the Public Schools.* Eugene, Ore: University of Oregon, Center for the Advanced Study of Educational Administration.

Chapman, C., Ainscow, M., Bragg, J., Gunter, H., Hull, J., Mongon, D., Muijs, D. and West, M. (2008) Emerging patterns of school leadership: Current practice and future directions. *A Research Report Prepared by the University of Manchester for the National College of School Leadership.* Nottingham: NCSL.

Chapman, J. (2002) *System Failure.* London: Demos.

Chitty, C. (2002) The role and status of LEAs: Post-war pride and *fin de siecle* uncertainty, *Oxford Review of Education,* Vol. 28 Nos. 2 & 3, 261–273.

Clarke, J. and Newman, J. (1997) *The Managerial State: Power, Politics and the Ideology in the Remaking of Social Welfare.* London: Sage.

Coleman, A. (2006), modified (2009) *Collaborative Leadership in Extended Schools. Leading in a Multidisciplinary Environment.* Nottingham: NCSL.

Cox, C. B. and Dyson, A. E. (1969a) *Black Paper Two: The Crisis in Education.* London: Critical Quarterly.

—. (1969b) *Fight for Education: A Black Paper.* London: Critical Quarterly.

Crawford, M. (2007) Emotional coherence in primary school headship, *Educational Management Administration Leadership,* Vol. 35, No. 4, 521–534.

Cuban, L. (1988) *The Managerial Imperative and the Practice of Leadership in Schools.* Albany, NY: State University of New York Press.

Day, C; Harris, A; Hadfield, M; Tolley, H. and Beresford, J. (2000) *Leading Schools in Times of Change.* Buckingham, Open University Press.

Department for Children Schools and Families (DCSF) (2007) *The Children's Plan: Building a 21st Century Schools System.* London: TSO.

—. (2009) *Your Child, Your Schools, Our Future: Building a 21st Century Schools System*. Cmnd 7588, London: HMSO.

Department for Education (DfE) (1992a) *Choice and Diversity: A New Framework for Schools*. Cmnd 2021, London: HMSO.

—. (1992b) *Education (Schools Act)*. London: HMSO.

—. (2010a) *Academies Act*. London: HMSO.

—. (2010b) *The Importance of Teaching*.White Paper. London: HMSO.

Department for Education (DfE) and Department for Business Innovation and Skills (BIS) (2010) *National Curriculum Assessments in England at Key Stage 2 2009/10* (Revised). Available online www.education.gov.uk/rsgateway/DB/SFR/s000975/index.shtml. Accessed 26 February 2011.

Department for Education and Employment (DfEE) (1996) *Self Government for Schools*. Cmnd. 3315. London: HMSO.

—. (1997a) *Excellence in Schools*. White Paper Cmnd 3681. London: HMSO.

—. (1997b) *From Targets to Action: Guidance to Support Effective Target-Setting in Schools*. London: HMSO.

—. (1998a) *Teachers: Meeting the Challenge of Change*. Green Paper. London: HMSO.

—. (1998b) *School Standards and Framework Act*. London: HMSO.

—. (1998c) *The National Literacy Strategy*. London: DfEE.

—. (1998d) *The National Numeracy Strategy*. London: DfEE.

Department for Education and Employment (DfEE) and Qualifications and Curriculum Agency (QCA) (1999) *The National Curriculum Handbook for Secondary Teachers in England*. London: HMSO.

Department of Education and Science (DES) (1944) *The Education Act*. London: HMSO.

—. (1980) *The Education Act*. London: HMSO.

—. (1985a) *Better Schools*. White Paper Cmnd 9649. London: HMSO, March.

—. (1985b) *Quality in Schools: Evaluation and Appraisal*. London: HMSO.

—. (1987) *The Education (School Teachers, Pay and Conditions) Order*. London: HMSO.

—. (1988) *The Education Reform Act*. London: HMSO.

—. (1990) *Developing School Management: The Way Forward*. London: HMSO.

Department for Education and Skills (DfES) (2001a) *Schools Achieving Success*. White Paper Cmnd 5230. London: HMSO.

—. (2001b) *Schools: Building on Success, Raising Standards, Promoting Diversity, Achieving Results*. Green Paper CM 5050. London: HMSO.

—. (2002a) *Education Act*. London: HMSO

—. (2003a) *Every Child Matters*. London: HMSO.

—. (2003b) *Excellence and Enjoyment. A Strategy for Primary Schools*. London: DfES.

—. (2003c) *National Agreement on Raising Standards and Tackling Workload: A National Agreement*. London: DfES.

—. (2003d) *Primary Leadership Programme: Collaborative Leadership for Improving Teaching and Learning in English and Mathematics*. London: DfES.

—. (2003e) *The London Challenge – Transforming London Secondary Schools*. London: DfES.

—. (2004a) *The Children's Act*. London: DfES.

—. (2004b) *End to End Review for the National College of School Leadership*. London: HMSO.

—. (2004c) *National Standards for Headteachers*. London: DfES.

—. (2005a) *Extended Schools: Access to Opportunities and Services for All: A Prospectus*. London: DfES.

—. (2005b) *Higher Standards Better Schools for All. More Choice for Parents and Pupils*. London: DfES.

—. (2006) *The Education and Inspections Act*. London: DfES.

—. (2007) *Governance Guidance for Sure Start Children's Centres and Extended Schools*. London: DfES.

Department for Education and Skills (DfES) and the Innovations Unit (2005) *Practitioner Guide: An Introduction to School Federations*. London: DfES.

Department for Education and Skills (DfES) and Office for Standards in Education (OFSTED) (2004) *A New Relationship with Schools*. London: DfES.

Dimmock, C. and Walker, A. (2000) Developing comparative and international educational leadership and management: A cross cultural model, *School Leadership and Management*, Vol. 20, No. 2, 143–160.

Docking, J. (2000) What is the solution? An overview of national policies for schools 1979–99, in J. Docking (ed.), *New Labour's Policies for Schools: Raising the Standard?* London: David Fulton, 21–42.

Earley, P. and Weindling, D. (2006) Consultant leadership – a new role for headteachers? *School Leadership and Management*, Vol. 26, No. 1, 37–53.

Elkins, T. and Elliott, J. (2004) Competition and Control: The impact of government regulation on teaching and learning in English schools, *Research Papers in Education*, Vol. 19, No. 1, 15–30.

Elmore, R. (2005) Accountable leadership, *The Educational Forum*, Vol. 69, Winter, 134–142.

Etzioni, A. (1969) *The Semi-Professionals and Their Organization*. New York: Macmillan.

Farrell, C. and Morris, J. (2003) The neo-bureaucratic state: Professionals managers and professional managers in schools, general practices and social work, *Organisation*, Vol. 10, No. 1, 129–156.

Fidler, B. and Atton, T. (2004) *The Headship Game: The Challenges of Contemporary School Leadership*. London: Routledge Falmer.

Fullan, M. (2005) *Leadership and Sustainability. System Leaders in Action*. London: Sage.

Garrett, V. (1997) Managing change, in Davies, B. and Ellison, L. (eds), *School Leadership for the 21st Century: A Competency and Knowledge Approach*. London: Routledge Falmer, 95–117.

Glatter, R. (2006) Leadership and organization in education: Time for a re-orientation? *School Leadership and Management*, Vol. 26, No. 1, 69–83.

Goleman, D. (1995) *Emotional Intelligence*. New York: Bantam Books.

Gorard, S. (2006) Value-added is of little value, *Journal of Education Policy*, Vol. 21, No. 2, 235–243.

Gronn, P. (2003) *The New Work of Educational Leaders: Changing Leadership Practice in the Era of School Reform*. Paul Chapman. London: Sage.

Gunter, H. (2008) Policy and workforce reform in England, *Educational Management Administration and Leadership*, Vol. 36, No. 2, 253–270.

Hargreaves, A. (2001) *Changing Teachers, Changing Times*. London: Continuum International Publishing Group.

Hargreaves, D. H. (2003) *Education Epidemic: Transforming Secondary Schools through Innovation Networks*. London: Demos.

—. (2010) *Creating a Self-Improving School System*. Nottingham: National College for Leadership of School and Children's Services.

Harris, A. (2005) Leading from the chalk-face: An overview of school leadership, *Leadership*, Vol. 1, 73–87.

—. (2008) Distributed leadership: According to the evidence, *Journal of Educational Administration*, Vol. 46, No. 2, 172–188.

—. (2009) Distributed leadership: Evidence and implications, in Tony Bush, Les Bell and David Middlewood (eds), *The Principles of Educational Leadership and Management*, 2nd edn, 55–69. London: Sage.

Harris, A., Brown, A., and Abbott, I. (2006) Executive leadership: Another lever in the system? *School Leadership and Management*, Vol. 26, No. 4, 397–409.

Hartley, D. (2003) New economy, new pedagogy? *Oxford Review of Education*, Vol. 29, No. 1, 81–94.

Hatcher, R. (2005) The distribution of leadership and power in schools, *British Journal of Sociology of Education*, Vol. 26, No. 2, 253–267.

—. (2006) Privatization and sponsorship: The re-agenting of the school system in England, *Journal of Education Policy*, Vol. 21, No. 5, 599–619.

Hatcher, R. and Troyna, B. (1994) The 'Policy Cycle': A ball by ball account, *Journal of Education Policy*, Vol. 9, No. 2, 155–170.

Heifetz, R. A. (1994) *Leadership Without Easy Answers*. Harvard, MA: Belknap Press.

Higham, R., Hopkins, D. and Matthews, P. (2009) *System Leadership in Practice*. London: Routledge Falmer.

Hill, R. (2010) *Chain Reactions: A Thinkpiece on the Development of Chains of Schools in the English School System*. Nottingham: National College for Leadership of School and Children's Services.

Hill, R. and Matthews, P. (2008) *Schools Leading Schools: The Power and Potential of National Leaders of Education*. Nottingham: National College for School Leadership.

—. (2010) *Schools Leading Schools11: The Growing Impact of National Leaders of Education*. Nottingham: National College for Leadership of School and Children's Services.

Hopkins, D. (2005) *Every School a Great School: Meeting the Challenge of Large Scale, Long Term Educational Reform*, inaugurate lecture for The London Centre for Leadership in Learning, Institute of Education, 30 June 2005, *iNet series*, Specialist Schools Trust, London.

—. (2006) *A Short Primer on System Leadership*. Paper given at The International Conference *International perspectives on School Leadership for Systemic Improvement*. OECD 6 July 2006.

House, R. J. (1977) A 1976 theory of charismatic leadership, in Hunt, J. G. and Larson, L. L. (eds), *Leadership: The Cutting Edge*. Carbondale, IL: Southern Illinois University Press, 189–207.

House of Commons (2008) *Testing and Assessment: Fifth Special Report of the Children, Schools and Families Committee*, Session 2007–2008. London: TSO.

Hoyle, E. and Wallace, M. (2007) Educational reform: An ironic perspective, *Educational Management Administration and Leadership*, Vol. 35, No. 1, 9–27.

Husbands, C. (2001) Managing performance in performing schools, in D. Gleeson and C. Husbands (eds), *The Performing School: Managing Teaching and Learning in a Performance Culture*. London: Routledge Falmer, 7–19.

—. (2011) *The Coalition and Schools*. Green Templeton College Oxford lecture, 14 February 2011.

Kingdon, J. W. (2003) *Agendas, Alternatives and Public Policies*. New York: Addison-Wesley.

Kogan, M. (2002) The subordination of local government and the compliant society, *Oxford Review of Education*, Vol. 28, Nos. 2 and 3, 331–342.

Labour Party (1997) *New Labour. Because Britain Deserves Better*. Election Manifesto. London: Labour Party.

Learner, S. (2001) Soft-touch style but tough on standards, *Times Educational Supplement*, 14 September 2001. Available online www.tes.co.uk/article.aspx?storycode=351724. Accessed 21 November 2008.

Leggett, B. (1997) Pressures of managerialism and its implications, *Australian Journal of Education*, Vol. 41, No. 3, 276–288.

Leithwood, K., Day, C., Sammons, P., Harris, A. and Hopkins, D. (2006) *Seven Strong Claims about Successful School Leadership*. London: DfES.

—. (2007) Modified (2009) *Successful School Leadership: What It Is and How It Influences Pupil Learning*. Available online www.nationalcollege.org.uk/docinfo?id=21851&filename=successful-school-leadership-full.pdf. Accessed 31 January 2011.

Leithwood, K., Edge, K. and Jantzi, D. (1999) *Educational Accountability: The State of the Art*. Gütersloh. Germany: Bertelsmann Foundation Publishers.

Levin, B. (2003) Conceptualising educational reform, in Preedy et al. (eds), *Strategic Leadership and Educational Improvement*. London: Open University Press and Paul Chapman Publishing, 33–43.

—. (2010) Governments and education reform: some lessons from the last 50 years, *Journal of Education Policy*, Vol. 25, No. 6, 739–747.

MacBeath, J. (2008) Stories of compliance and subversion in a prescriptive policy environment, *Educational Management Administration and Leadership*, Vol. 36, No. 1, 123–148.

March, J. and Olsen, J. (1989) *Rediscovering Institutions: The Organizational Basis of Politics*. New York: Free Press.

Miliband, D. (Minister of State for School Standards, DfES) (2004) *Personalised Learning: Building a New Relationship with Schools*, address to *North of England Education Conference*. Belfast, Ireland, 8 January 2004. Department for Education and Skills. Available online www.education.gov.uk/publications/eOrderingDownload/personalised-learning.pdf. Accessed 9 April 2007.

Moos, L., Krejsler, J. and Kofod, K. K. (2008) Successful principals: Telling or selling? On the importance of context for school leadership, *International Journal of Leadership in Education*, October, Vol. 11, No. 4, 341–352.

Moore, A., George, R. and Halpin, D. (2002) The developing role of the headteacher in English schools: Management, leadership and pragmatism, *Educational Management and Administration*, Vol. 30, No. 2, 175–198.

Morris, E. (2001) *Professionalism and Trust – The Future of Teachers and Teaching*, A speech by the secretary of state for education to the Social Market Foundation, 12 November. London: SMF.

Mourshed, M., Chijioke, C. and Barber, M. (2010) *How the World's Most Improved School Systems Keep Getting Better*. London: McKinsey & Co. Available online http://ssomckinsey.darbyfilms. com/reports/schools/How-the-Worlds-Most-Improved-School-Systems-Keep-Getting-Better_ Download-version_Final.pdf. Accessed 28 February 2011.

Mulford, B. (2003) *School Leaders: Changing Roles and Impact on Teacher and School Effectiveness*. A paper commissioned by the Education and Training Policy Division, OECD, for the Activity *Attracting, Developing and Retaining Effective Teachers*. April.

National Association of Headteachers (NAHT) (2010) *Gove Tells OFSTED to 'ditch' the Self Evaluation Form*. 24 September 2010. London: NAHT. Available online www.naht.org.uk/welcome/resources/ key-topics/inspections/gove-tells-OFSTED-to-ditch-the-sef-in-england/. Accessed 21 January 2011.

National College for Leadership of Schools and Children's Services (NC) (2009a) *National College Remit Letter 2009-2010*. Available online www2.nationalcollege.org.uk/download?id=14740. Accessed 15 December 2010.

—. (2009b) *School Leadership Today*. National College Publishing. Available online www. nationalcollege.org.uk/docinfo?id=21843&filename=school-leadership-today.pdf Accessed 3 March 2011

—. (2010) *Executive Heads*. National College Publishing. Available online www.nationalcollege.org.uk/ docinfo?id=140381&filename=executive-heads-full-report.pdf. Accessed 29 April 2011.

—. (2011a) *National Leaders of Education and National Support Schools*. National College Publishing. Available online www.nationalcollege.org.uk/index/professional-development/national-leaders- of-education.htm. Accessed 31 January 2011.

—. (2011b) National College Remit Letter 2011–2012. Available online www.nationalcollege.org.uk/ docinfo?id=146332&filename=remit-letter-2011-12.pdf. Accessed 20 April 2011.

National College for School Leadership (NCSL) (2005) *Leadership in Complex Schools: Advice to the Secretary of State*. Nottingham: www.nationalcollege.org.uk/docinfo?id=14952&filename=leaders hip-in-complex-schools.pdf. Accessed 10 May 2011.

—. (2006) *Succession Planning Formal Advice to the Secretary of State*. Nottingham: NCSL. Available online www.ncsl.org.uk/ncsl-succession-planning-advice.pdf. Accessed 25 October 2007.

—. (2007) *Primary Leadership: Advice to the Secretary of State*. Nottingham: NCSL. Available online www. ncsl.org.uk/media-ad4-e3-advice-to-sos-primary-leadership-oct07.pdf. Accessed 20 January 2008.

Office for Standards in Education (OFSTED) (1996) *The Annual Report of Her Majesty's Chief Inspector of Schools: Standards and Quality in Education 1994/1995*. London: OFSTED.

—. (2002a) *The National Literacy Strategy: The First Four Years 1998–2002*. London: OFSTED.

—. (2002b) *The National Numeracy Strategy: The First Three Years 1999–2002*. London: OFSTED.

Plowden Report (1967) *Children and Their Primary Schools*. London: HMSO.

Pont, B., Nusche, D. and Moorman, H. (2008) *Improving School Leadership, Volume 1: Policy and Practice*. Paris: OECD.

Powell, J. L. and Edwards, M. (2005) Surveillance and morality: Revisiting the Education Reform Act (1988) in the United Kingdom, *Surveillance & Society*, Vol. 3, No. 1, 96–106.

Price Waterhouse Coopers (2001) *Teachers Workload Study*. London: DfES.

Price Waterhouse Coopers (2007) *Independent Study into School Leadership*. London: DfES.

Robinson, S. (2009) *Primary Headteachers: New Leadership Roles Inside and Outside the School*. Birmingham City University: Unpublished PhD thesis.

—. (2011) Primary headteachers: New leadership roles inside and outside the school, *Educational Management Administration & Leadership*, Vol. 39, No. 1, 63–83.

Rose, J. (2009) *Independent Review of the Primary Curriculum: Final Report*. Nottingham: DCSF.

Rutherford, D. (2004) Headteachers' reflections on primary headship from 1988–2003: An exploratory study, *Journal of Educational Administration*, Vol. 43, No. 3, 278–294.

Ryan, C. (2011) Interview with the author, March 2011.

Scott, D. (2000) *Reading Educational Research and Policy Texts*. London: Routledge.

Simkins, T. (2005) Leadership in education, *Educational Management & Leadership*, Vol. 33, No. 1, 9–26.

Southworth, G. (2008) Primary school leadership today and tomorrow, *School Leadership and Management*, Vol. 28, No. 5, 413–434.

Spillane, J. (2006) *Distributed Leadership*. Chicago: Jossey-Bass.

Spillane, J., Diamond, B., Sherer, J. and Coldren, A. (2005) Distributing leadership, in Coles, M. and Southworth G. (eds), *Developing Leadership, Creating the Schools of Tomorrow*. London: Oxford University Press, 37–50.

Spring, J. (2008) Research on globalization and education, *Review of Educational Research*, Vol. 78, 330–363.

Stewart, W. (2009) Academics demolish 'useless' CVA system, *Times Educational Supplement*, 27 February. Available online www.tes.co.uk/article.aspx?storycode=6009334. Accessed 10 March 2009.

Teacher Training Agency (TTA) (1997) *Training Curriculum and Standards for New Teachers*. London: TTA.

—. (1998) *National Standards for Headteachers*. London: TTA.

Times Educational Supplement (TES) Heads cool on Gove's pledge to shift teacher training into schools (24 December 2010) www.tes.co.uk/article.aspx?storycode=6066489. Accessed 3 January 2011.

Thomson, P. (2008) Headteacher critique and resistance: A challenge for policy, and for leadership/management scholars, *Journal of Educational Administration and History*, Vol. 40, No. 2, 85–100.

Tomlinson, S. (2001) *Education in a Post-Welfare Society*. Buckingham: Open University Press.

Wade, P., McCrone, T. and Rudd, P. (2007) *National Evaluation of the Primary Leadership Programme*. Research Brief 820, National Foundation for Educational Research, London: DfES Publications.

Wallace, M. (2001) Sharing leadership of schools through teamwork: A justifiable risk? *Educational Management and Administration*, Vol. 29, No. 2, 153–167.

Walsh, K. (1994) Marketing and public sector management, *European Journal of Marketing*, Vol. 28, No. 3, 63–71.

Webb, P. T. (2006) The choreography of accountability, *Journal of Education Policy*, Vol. 21, No. 2, 201–214.

Woodhead, C. (1999) Platform: Why inspections set you free, *Times Educational Supplement*, 14 May. Available online www.tes.co.uk/article.aspx?storycode=311263. Accessed 2 June 2009.

Woods, P., Jeffrey, B., Troman, G. and Boyle, M. (1997) *Restructuring Schools, Reconstructing Teachers: Responding to Change in the Primary School*. Buckingham: Open University Press.

Yukl, G. (2002) *Leadership in Organisations*, 5th edn. Upper Saddle River, NJ: Prentice-Hall.

Index